RAFFI

(Hakob Melik-Hagobian, c. 1835-1888)

SPARKS

TWELVE SELECTIONS

translated by Donald Abcarian

Gomidas Institute
London

GOMIDAS INSTITUTE - ARMENIAN LITERATURE IN TRANSLATION

Published by the Gomidas Institute, 2021.

ISBN 978-1-909382-61-9

For further comments and inquiries please contact:

Gomidas Institute
42 Blythe Rd.
London, W14 0HA
Email: *info@gomidas.org*
Web: *www.gomidas.org*

TABLE OF CONTENTS

Translator's Preface

Sparks (Gaidzer) is Raffi's longest novel, a multi-branched narrative divided into two volumes and running over seven hundred pages. After *Jalaleddin* and *The Fool*, it was Raffi's final and most ambitious novel to address the grave implications of the Russo-Turkish War of 1877-78 for the future of Armenia. It was published in the troubling aftermath of the Treaty of Berlin which, in its final settlement of that war, had shunted Armenian aspirations and sacrifices aside and raised the specter of what became known for decades to follow as the "Armenian Question." The heroes Raffi brought to life in its pages sparked intense controversy in Armenian circles of the day and influenced the ensuing struggle for national liberation. Following its publication, Raffi was branded a "nihilist," his home was invaded by state police, all his manuscripts were taken, and he was subjected to house arrest. It was against this background that the novel was greeted with popular acclaim on its first appearance in Tiflis in 1883.

Farhad is the narrator and the novel is cast as his memoir. These selections, comprising about a seventh of the whole work, focus on the arc of his life from the end of childhood to the momentous adventures of early manhood. They are presented in chronological order. Significantly, the first selection depicts the primitive village school which was, physically and philosophically, the point of departure for the central characters of the novel and will remain a key point of reference throughout. It represents everything the protagonists will struggle against as the novel unfolds. Farhad is a younger member of this group and, in relationship to them, is cast as the eternal initiate or greenhorn. All of them were his comrades, and all of them were united in their burning resentment of the coercion and stifling ignorance imposed on them by their abusive, tyrannical teacher. One day, all the leading personalities of this group suddenly fail to appear at school and seem to vanish from the face of the earth. After the lapse of many years, under unexpected and mysterious circumstances, Farhad encounters them again and is given a warm welcome back into their company. Among them is Aslan, whom Farhad remembers with particular respect from school days. In time, Aslan will set out on a horseback trek to Van to explore key sites of ancient Armenian history. He accepts Farhad as a sidekick and, with the clandestine purpose of preparing the ground for a decisive national liberation struggle, he leads the way to Van in the guise of a European doctor and antiquarian.

In presenting this set of translations from Sparks I wish to acknowledge my deep gratitude to Seda Khachaturian, Rita Gragossian and the other descendants of the great writer's family who graciously offered me their guidance and support and inspired me to see this project through to completion.

Donald Abcarian,
Berkeley, California
January, 2021

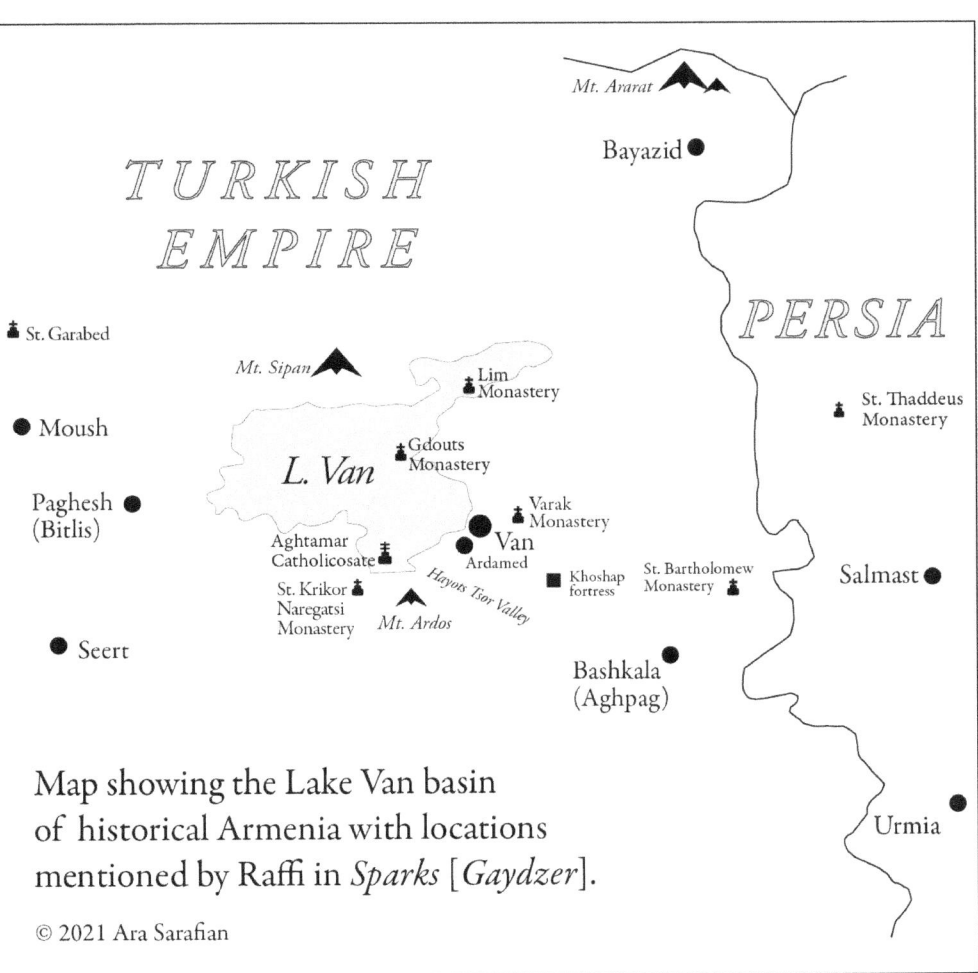

TURKISH
EMPIRE

PERSIA

Mt. Ararat

Bayazid ●

St. Garabed

Mt. Sipan

Lim
Monastery

St. Thaddeus
Monastery

Moush ●

Gdouts
Monastery

L. Van

Paghesh ●
(Bitlis)

Varak
Monastery

Aghtamar
Catholicosate

Van
Ardamed

St. Krikor
Naregatsi
Monastery

Hayots Tsor Valley

Mt. Ardos

Khoshap
fortress

St. Bartholomew
Monastery

Salmast ●

Seert ●

Bashkala
(Aghpag) ●

Map showing the Lake Van basin
of historical Armenia with locations
mentioned by Raffi in *Sparks* [*Gaydzer*].

Urmia ●

© 2021 Ara Sarafian

SPARKS

TWELVE SELECTIONS

School

Our school was a spare room in Father Todik's house. It was right up against the barn and practically a part of it. About forty of us squeezed into that stifling little hole and, on top of that, had to share the space with three newborn calves that Father Todik kept tethered there. There wasn't enough fuel to make fires in winter but we made do by simply opening the windows between us and the barn and letting the steamy warmth of the animals flow in. It rolled in like a fog and got our room as hot as a bathhouse. Ah, how comfortable we were!

But the summers were another matter. They were unbearable due to the accumulation of manure in the barn. There we were, trapped between the obnoxious stench of the barn and the invasion of all kinds of microscopic vermin. Only God knew how the bites of such tiny creatures could cause so much pain!

As bare as a Turkish mosque, without so much as a bench, a chair, or even a table, that little room was where all the subjects were taught, from the lowest to the highest, from the alphabet to that enormous tome that I could barely carry back to the chapter house. There was no flooring and most of us sat cross-legged on the damp earth with nothing beneath us but grass matting. Father Todik sat on a goat skin and some of the wealthier students sat on small rugs they brought from home.

The only sign that this deathly, dreary cell was a school was the *falaka**** and the pile of freshly cut switches beside it. I don't know how many times we stole the infernal thing away and smashed it to bits. And yet it was always there, always. . . Our bare feet would be tied to it and hoisted up, then our soles would be whipped until we went limp and passed out. That was what the falaka was all about. And the worst part was that a classmate did the whipping. If he balked at the job or went too easy on us, he himself would receive the same punishment.

Class began early in the morning with Father Todik sitting in the corner with a little bookstand near him and wrapped like a shaman in an

---

*. The *falaka* or *bastinado* is the practice of beating the soles of the feet for punishment or the equipment used therein.

aura of holiness. We would take turns presenting ourselves to him. We first kissed his hand, then knelt down, placed our books on his bookstand and recited our lesson for the day. If we completely failed the lesson, the dreaded falaka was waiting for us. For small mistakes the usual punishment was a blow to the palm of the hand with an oar-shaped paddle, a terrible and ungodly punishment.

Engraved in the paddle were the complete directions for properly administering the punishment, which were taken from ancient scriptures. These paddles were specially made for each teacher. According to Father Todik, he had received his from his own teacher as a reward for being such a good student.

I remember to this day each and every punishment inflicted on us with such absurd cruelty. For instance, we would be forced to stand and hold a brick or heavy church book over our heads for hours like Hindu fakirs. Our arms would tire and our nerves would weaken, but to no avail. The worst part of it was that we were forced to stand on one foot, usually the left, and never put the other one down. One of our classmates would be stationed next to us with a whip in his hand to monitor our terrible ordeal and ready to whip us if our other foot went down. I became so used to this particular punishment that I could stand like a goose for long periods of time.

There were other punishments, as well. For instance, we had to come to school on totally empty stomachs, without even having a bite of bread. Tea or coffee were unknown to us at that time, but we would be severely punished even if we had had a little *tahn*[*] or *madzoon*[†] before school.

"You can't learn a thing on a full stomach. As soon as you eat, your intelligence flies out the window," Father Todik insisted, and, so saying, he cited great ascetics and vartabeds[‡] who had authored a host of books on empty stomachs.

We made sure to obey his rule because it was simply impossible to deceive him. He knew with devilish cunning if any of us had broken our fast. The first thing he did each morning was closely examine the tongue of anyone he suspected of breaking the fast. A person who has fasted will have a gleaming layer of white froth on his tongue, but it is washed away

*. *Tahn* – a cold refreshing beverage made of diluted yoghurt mixed with chopped cucumber, parsely, mint, etc.
†. *Madzoon* (Armenian) or yoghurt.
‡. A *vartabed* is a learned monk who engages in scholarship and teaching.

by eating and then the tongue will be pink. This is why we not only kept the fast but were even afraid to wash our faces for fear we might accidentally get some water in our mouth and flush away the white froth. So, until noon we had to make do on totally empty stomachs, our heads swimming and our eyes going dim – and we didn't learn a thing.

For a clock we had the shadow that crept up the wall. When it reached a certain point we knew it was noon. Then and only then were we allowed to have a bite to eat. But, oh, what an agony waiting for that moment! The sun seemed as heartless as our teacher, going slowly, ever so slowly, the shadow barely moving at all . . .

We ate our lunch in the classroom. Everyone brought their own lunches and shared the choicest parts of them with Father Todik. This gave him the biggest and most varied lunch of all. Not only that, he had enough left over to share with his wife and children in the evening.

Though we were allowed a couple of hours to relax after lunch, playing, as such, was strictly forbidden and was regarded as a form of mischief that violated the norms of modesty and composure. A pupil was supposed to remain quiet and meek. Anyone found playing – let alone playing with toys, which was even worse – would be severely punished. To this end there were spot inspections of our pockets. Sons of wealthy families were, however, spared these harsh measures and given a lot of slack. They always sat in the front row and enjoyed complete impunity, even if they beat up their poorer schoolmates in the yard. A boy named Alo was one of these, the son of our town's wealthiest man. His father financed the royal mint located in our town and was its director. In that era Persia had its money minted in several larger towns, and the financing of those enterprises was in the hands of certain rich families. This role was hereditary and passed down from generation to generation within certain families called 'sarafs.' Alo was one of the worst students in our school and no one but Father Todik had any use for him. When someone had to be punished, he was always the first to volunteer for the privilege of administering it. He took special pleasure in beating his schoolmates and Father Todik never once deprived him of the opportunity . . . He would come to school every day with a different book that he brought from home and tell Father Todik, "My father said to use this book for today's lesson."

"Fine, then this is the book we'll use," Father Todik would answer.

One day I finally had my fill of this and said to Alo, "You still have to sound out each letter when you read the Psalms. How are you going to read that whole book?"

"Well, my father's a very important man," he said proudly.

"I know, but you still have a long way to go before you can read a book like that."

"What are you talking about? My father said to bring it to school so I can be the top student in my class."

"Like he's the number one man in town?" I said with a laugh.

Suddenly I felt a slap on my face. I shot back with a powerful punch. The little coward immediately ran to Father Todik and tattled on me. You can imagine the terrible punishment in store for me for having the nerve to strike the son of the richest man in town. That was something that couldn't be allowed. It was from that day that I conceived a hatred for anything that smacked of royal privilege or those who profited from it. . .

There was plenty of reason for the privileges the rich pupils enjoyed: on feast days they brought offerings of wine, brandy, butter, cheese, and so on for Father Todik. Their fathers would send him special gifts when they had finished reading one book and were ready for the next.

But we were poor and my mother could barely pay the monthly tuition. In lieu of providing Father Todik with special gifts, I had to do various household chores for him and was never given a moment's rest from morning to night. I hauled water from the spring. I went out into the fields to gather grass for the cows to eat and held them still while his wife milked them. After dinner, if there was nothing else to do, I had to sit next to Father Todik and whisk away the flies until he had fallen sweetly asleep . . .

On days when Father Todik had baptisms or weddings to perform he would turn them into holidays for himself. But for us they would be days of death. Some of our older schoolmates, who had been trained to assist him, would accompany him to the ceremonies and carry his mantle, the *Mashdots*,[*] the censer, and other liturgical items. Far from being able to breathe a little easier on those days, our lot became even worse. On the assumption that we would act up in some way when he was gone, Father Todik devised a fiendishly clever way to keep us in line. He made us sit far apart from each other with the long fringes of our clothing spread out

[*]. *Mashdots* or the prayerbook of the Armenian church.

around us on the ground, then sprinkled sand over them and pressed a pattern into the sand with a special seal made for the purpose. Imagine our situation, forced to sit motionless on the bare floor for hours and hours to avoid disturbing the pattern and being severely punished when he returned.

And I had more than my share of such punishment. Good Lord, what was I to do? Could I just sit there as if I were dead? I'd sometimes get bitten by a flea, or bothered by a fly, or have some other need . . .

Father Todik would finally come back in a totally drunken state. On finding my seal broken, he would be all too ready to subject me to the accursed falaka – or else have me kneel with bare knees on bits of broken brick. And once again, I had to remain perfectly frozen in place . . .

And then there were days of general punishment. We had a few holidays during the year, the biggest being one week each for Easter and Christmas. When we returned to school after these holidays, Father Todik would punish everyone the same with the falaka. Why? Because some of us must have done something naughty while we were away and, because it was impossible to find out who had done so, it was necessary for the innocent to be punished along with the guilty . . . This barbarity served another purpose, as well: Like an experienced equestrian who gives his horse a whiplash when he mounts to stimulate it and focus its attention, in the same way Father Todik intended by hitting us to rouse and prime our mental energies after a wild and carefree vacation and thus prepare us for the rigors of school . . .

Father Todik wasn't a malevolent man. On the contrary, he was quite decent, but all his punishments stemmed from his understanding of what being a good teacher meant. He was convinced that without corporal punishment, without pressure, a child could learn nothing. He had as much faith in the falaka as in the various talismans and magical rites with which he had achieved such remarkable results . . .

When I told my mother about my sufferings at school, she thought the same way as Father Todik: "Until you learn to take a whipping and put up with pressure, you won't learn a thing," she would say. But if that were true why, after all that torture, had I still learned nothing?

I wasn't a dull-witted boy. In fact, I had a very sharp mind. For instance, when my grandmother told me a tale I would effortlessly remember it word for word. And when an *ashough*[*] visited town to sing and tell his stories, I learned it all right away. So why was I so dull in school? Why did all my intelligence vanish there? I understood my grandmother's tales and the songs of the ashough. I learned them well. But the lessons Father Todik gave us were unintelligible and didn't even seem to be in Armenian. Though I studied them day and night, nothing stuck. As soon as Father Todik's eyes met mine, I became terrified and confused and forgot everything . . .

So abject was I in mind and spirit, so deadened in me were my youthful energies that I believed Father Todik when he said, "You devil's bastard, you'll never amount to anything!"

Father Todik started teaching me the alphabet. It's as if that primer is still before my eyes with its large printed letters and in one corner a picture of the Cross with the words, "Help me, Oh Cross!" beneath it.

For many months I crossed myself and repeated those words. Father Todik said that without crossing yourself you can't learn anything. But it seemed that even the Cross foiled my mind and was powerless to instill any sense or intelligence in me . . .

I haven't been able to rid myself, even to this day, of the unpleasant feeling that studying the alphabet left me with . . . It seemed that every letter was a dragon about to swallow me up . . . and my sleep was troubled at night . . . I was as tormented in my dreams as I was at school.

My teacher had a wife and two children, Stepan and little Sona. Stepan, the oldest, was always still and mute. With a colorless face and lifeless eyes, he was a dull-witted child. You could hardly look at him without feeling sorry for him.

Despite the fact that Father Todik was the senior priest for a parish of seven hundred homes; despite the fact that he was also official functionary for the prelate of the diocese, all of which brought him considerable earnings (not to mention his job as a teacher); despite all of this, his life was marked by poverty. A few gloomy rooms with white plaster walls, a cramped yard surrounded by low walls, this constituted his inglorious residence; a place where deep sadness reigned, along with everlasting dust and filth. The neighbors took his destitution as the sign of someone by nature averse to selfish ambition and worldly pleasure. This might have been so, were it not that misers live in a similar mortifying desolation and that there are dervishes who similarly cast an aura of poverty over the

---

*. An *ashough* is a traveling troubadour, minstrel, story-teller.

superstitious populace, though beneath many a dervish's tattered cloak lies a greedy and grasping heart. . .

During the last several years, my mother had been unable to pay Father Todik my tuition, and I had to take on the burden of countless domestic tasks around his house instead. This left me no time to do my lessons. From morning to night, I had to knock myself out meeting the various demands Father Todik and his wife placed on me. That left me only evenings free, but by that time I couldn't study because there wasn't enough oil for the lamps and everyone went to bed early.

But I did have one consolation in all this hell, Father Todik's daughter, Sona, an angel who relieved the bitterness of my lot. As for what it was that bound my heart to that delightful being, I couldn't understand – and to this day, I still don't understand.

Sona helped me a great deal, especially with my chores. When I went out into the fields to reap hay for the cows, she went with me and would say:

"Sit down somewhere and study your lesson, Farhad, I'll reap the hay for you."

"You can't do it all by yourself, Sona, you'll get too tired," I would say.

She would smile at me and say with angelic kindness, "No, I can. Sit down and study so my father doesn't punish you."

Though she wanted to do whatever she could to allow me time for my studies, she couldn't, because she was forbidden to be with me. So I had to go sadly into the field all by myself and reap the hay.

Thus passed seven whole years, a mystical number that spanned my childhood and earliest sufferings. . . In the course of those seven years I passed through all the levels of learning, that is, through everything an advanced pupil was expected to master in those days: the Psalms, the breviary, the Gospel, the Old Testament, the Nareg,[*] and even that enormous book that from early childhood was very hard for me to lift up. I was able to write and read what I had written and learned many of the grammatical rules of classical Armenian. The only subjects that remained inaccessible to me were science and magic. These my teacher kept to himself as specialties. I could only study those after serving him for ten or twenty years.

---

*. Nareg is the holy "Book of Lamentations" by Saint Gregory of Nareg (Sourp Krikor Naregatsi, 10th century).

I was ten years old when I started school. That was twelve years earlier. By now I was a young man, but Father Todik still treated me like a child and meted out the same punishments: the same falaka, the same paddle blow to the hand, the same kneeling on bits of brick. . . In a word, nothing had changed as far as punishment was concerned. But what was truly remarkable was how used to it I became. So inwardly dead was I to my own honor and self-respect that I put up with it all like a beast of burden that mutely receives the cruel blows of its master. But there was one memorable exception to this pattern.

It was the time of the Easter holiday, and none of the pupils in Father Todik's school was up to memorizing the entire Book of Daniel to recite in church on Easter Sunday. This book was usually recited by pupils from rich families, and for this privilege their parents would make a sizable donation to the church. The teacher in charge of this recitation would have the chosen pupil recite the book by heart to prove how advanced his pupils were in their studies. But who among the pupils from rich homes would be able to memorize the entire Book of Daniel?

They had all been studying and studying since the beginning of Lent but, with Easter rapidly approaching, no matter whom my teacher asked to recite it, none could, and he had no choice but to ask me. This was on Maundy Thursday, the day of Christ's passion and crucifixion. . . It would take an equal level of suffering to memorize the entire Book of Daniel in just one day's time! At midday on Holy Saturday Father Todik asked me how I was doing, but at that point I had only memorized three quarters of the book. I thought I'd have the chance to memorize the rest by the beginning of evening Mass, but Father Todik completely lost his patience and flew into a rage, assaulting me with a string of the vilest curses I had ever heard. At that point I couldn't take any more and gave vent to some rude words of my own.

"Why, you devil's offspring, I'll curse the hair on your head!" he bellowed in rage. But he didn't have any more time to spend on me and, instead, locked me up in the barn. He told me that's where I'd stay until he was finished with the evening services and that he would then come back and ring my neck.

The worst thing about it was that I had strictly kept the Lenten fast for the whole forty day period. I had gone to church morning, noon, and night and repeated all the prayers. That was the night I was supposed to go to church, attend Mass, and when "Holy Holy Holy" was sung, hold up the red Easter egg my mother had dyed for me and show the whole congregation that I had completed my fast. All of these pious intentions were blocked now and taken away from me even though I was alive with religious feeling and my heart was brimming with the ardor of faith. Each ceremony and every form of worship in the church held sacred meaning to me. It hurt me deeply to be barred from church. And, beyond that, I was tormented by another terrible resentment: I was the leading pupil in the school, yet pupils who were a hundred times inferior to me could freely go to church, take part in the ceremonies, give the responses, recite the verses, chant the prayers and thereby make their parents proud, while my poor mother would be denied the chance of even hearing the sound of my voice. So engrossed was I in all these thoughts that I entirely forgot about the punishment my teacher had threatened to give me when he returned. And what a stupendous contradiction! He was going to punish me and subject me to a barbarous beating after having stood as a priest before God's holy altar and announced, "Christ is risen from the dead, with His death He trampled death, with His resurrection he granted us life."

And my prison? I hadn't even paid it any attention in all my anxiety. Though it was only April, the heat was already setting in. The barn in which I was imprisoned was full of insects that bored into my body with their searing bites. On the one hand I was overwhelmed with the gaseous smell of manure, and on the other weak from hunger. Merciful God, what was I to do! The door was firmly locked and escape was impossible, yet putting up with that hell might be the death of me.

The sun had already set, and little by little the darkness was spreading in the barn. I felt like I was losing my mind and became panic stricken. Like an animal that has just fallen into an iron trap, I dashed from one side of my prison to the other, trying to scratch through the walls, pull down the posts, poke holes in the roof, break the door down, pry open the narrow window slots, all in an attempt to free myself. This struggle went on for several hours until, exhausted and weak, I collapsed on the floor and in that state was overtaken by all sorts of confused fantasies. The creatures that I had heard about in my grandmother's tales now came to life in my imagination: seven-headed dragons, demons with horns, devils with tails. They all crowded before my eyes and, I thought, the darkness will envelope everything, then they will come and strangle me. . .

As for how many hours I lay there in that state, I don't know, but all of a sudden I heard the door burst open. My whole body shivered with fear, but this didn't last long, for I saw that it was Sona who had come in like a visiting angel, a lantern in her hand. She helped me up, and her tender voice totally brought me to my senses again.

"Run away, Farhad! Run away while my father's gone. . ."

I wanted to kiss her for saving me, but she was gone like a wraith. . .

And I fled my prison, leaving behind once and for all my school, the hell of my torments, and my youth . . .

Old Friends

Having escaped from my prison I decided then and there never to return home again. I knew that if I went back my mother would just deliver me back to school and turn me over to my teacher again, uttering those same dreadful words: "His flesh is yours, his bone is mine." Now I knew what those words really meant.

It was dark when I escaped, and I was in such a desperate state I had no idea where to go or what to do. "Maybe I should just go and throw myself in the river and be done with my troubles," I thought.

I started wandering through the empty streets of the town in this distraught state. Everyone was inside now, having returned home from Easter services. They were gathering around their tables to enjoy their holiday meal together. The sacred smell of incense wafted from their houses and I could hear them singing hymns and exchanging the traditional Easter greeting, "Christ is risen from the dead." Yes, the God of love and peace was risen. . . But where were love and peace to be found? Where was the brotherhood I had heard so much about my entire life but had never seen? I went on wandering through the streets, a condemned fugitive with nowhere to go.

I was by now practically out of my mind with despair. I hardly heard or saw anything and felt totally cut off from the world. Without even knowing how I had got there I suddenly found myself at the river's edge and was about to throw myself in when I was stopped in my tracks by the sound of someone's voice:

"Hey, what are you doing there?"

The voice was very familiar, but due to the darkness and my distraught mental state I had trouble realizing who it was. "Don't you recognize me Farhad?"

"Oh, Garo! Dear friend! No, how could it be? Where did you come from? They said you. . ."

"But yes, it's me – Garo."

I was so happy I could hardly believe it. I clung to him. I kissed his neck, his face, his eyes and hands and blurted out everything I had been through.

"Have you completely lost your mind?" he said noticing the Book of Daniel that I was still unconsciously carrying under my arm. "What can I say?" I answered.

"Well, throw that damned pile in the river and be done with it," he said.

I did as he told me without another thought and as the book was swallowed up in the icy torrent of the river it seemed that all my troubles were carried off with it . . .

"Great! That's over with, now let's go," he said.

Garo had disappeared from our school twelve years earlier, but in those twelve years how he had changed! I had known him as a frail boy, but he was now a robust, imposing man. Though he was only four years older than I, he was much taller and already had a thick black moustache and bold, self-confident air.

"Where are we going?" I finally asked when we had left town a good distance behind us.

"I'm taking you where you'll get to see your old friends Aslan and Sako again. Surely you haven't forgotten them?"

"Aslan and Sako!" I cried with joy, barely able to contain myself.

"Yes, you'll be seeing them soon enough. But listen, Farhad, there's something I have to tell you. I didn't want to be seen by anyone ever again, but we happened to run into each other. I'm counting on you to keep it a secret. Can I?"

"But why?"

"I can't explain it now, but you'll find out soon enough."

"My lips are sealed," I answered.

"Good, that's the way it has to be."

Having gone more than half a mile through the wilderness we reached the site of some ancient ruins that my grandmother had told me all sorts of fabulous stories about. All that remained intact was a minaret that now, with the magical gleam of its bluish mosaics in the night, stood more beautiful than I ever remembered seeing it during the day. But because of the superstitious fears my grandmother's stories had instilled in me, I was afraid to approach it even in broad daylight, let alone now in the dead of night.

As we approached the minaret Garo let out a piercing whistle and was answered by a similar whistle from inside. At his urging I stepped inside. The interior was lit up with a bonfire burning in the middle of the floor.

It cast its purplish light up into the dome. A couple of men were grilling meat over it, with bread and wine set nearby. Some others were stretched out on the bare floor on one side.

Noticing Garo come in, the two men at the fire joined him and all three withdrew into the shadows and fell into hushed conversation. Their conversation went on for quite a while and I felt offended that no one seemed to notice me. I couldn't hear what they were talking about but, whatever it was, they didn't seemed very pleased and I thought they might be talking about me.

When they finished talking, one of them – a plump, lively fellow – came up to me. "Oh-ho! Where did you come from?" he asked.

I didn't care for his rudeness, but Garo stepped in:

"Don't tell me you don't recognize him, Sako!" Then turning to the rest of the group: "You see what a fine guest I've brought you? Guess who he is. I won't give you a hint." Only then did it become clear it wasn't me they had been talking about a few minutes earlier.

Sako drew near and looked me up and down. "It's Farhad as sure as I'm standing here. I'd recognize him anywhere. Ah, what a fine fellow you've turned into after all these years, isn't that so?"

"My goodness, it is Farhad after all!" said Aslan, coming up and giving me a big hug.

Aslan and the others had suddenly disappeared from Father Todik's school twelve years earlier and I had never heard why, or where they went.

Aslan was one of Father Todik's best students. He had always been kind to me and given me much of his time. He hadn't changed much, with his light blue eyes, his fair features, his serene expression and innocent smile.

"So. . . straight out of school to here, isn't that so?" he said with a smile. Before I could respond, Sako jumped in:

"Just look at him, Aslan, you can see it written all over his face. He's all sickly from being steeped in his ABCs night and day, isn't that so Farhad? Ah, how did I ever get out of that hole! I just threw the whole pile in the fireplace one day and left. . ."

Suddenly Garo's voice rang out inviting everyone to gather around the fire and have something to eat. The meal – nothing more than bread, cheese and onions – was carelessly set on a horse blanket spread on the ground.

"Sit next to me," said Garo.

I sat down beside him, but although I had eaten nothing all day I didn't have any appetite. My mind was too filled with the disturbing sequence of events I had just been through. But what a remarkable fate, to be sitting there after all those years reunited with my old friends, Aslan, Sako and Garo, who had disappeared from Father Todik's school many years before.

Garo's Speech

The bare mountain crags were dimming in the twilight and darkness spread through the canyons below. Only the great masses of golden clouds rolling through the sky high above shone brightly still, reflecting the last purple rays of the sun.

It was a beautiful evening, that hour of country life when the shepherd's song rings out so sweetly, when one's heart is touched by the far-off bleating of flocks and joyful whinnying of horses hurrying to their shelter for the night – the hour when gentle breezes caress one's face and whisper, "Breathe deeply of this fragrant air laden with the scents of the untold flowers I've gathered for you."

But I was impervious to such promptings. I had no ear for the zephyr's melody or the shepherd's song. I could only think of Maro. . .

Our return to the village would take a long time, because we took a different road than the one that had brought us. The road we chose for our return led to the farm owned by Haso, Hunter Avo's adoptive son.

Haso had made a shelter out of woven branches, the perfect lodging for a springtime night. Given the hour, we decided to spend the night there.

Haso lost no time building a great crackling fire in front of the shelter and it cast its light all around. It was only then that I saw my old friend clearly enough to recognize the renewal and transformation that time had brought about in him since school days. He had always been known as listless and lethargic in school and the other boys made fun of him. He was now a robust and very focused young man. What a difference tilling the soil had made in him, compared to learning ABC's from a priest! The latter had worn him down and robbed him of his childhood without offering his mind anything in return. The former had invigorated him and kept his father's house stocked with daily bread…

The village wasn't far from Haso's farm and the provisions Hunter Avo had promised were soon delivered – plentiful amounts of wine and bread. Everyone was famished by this time. The meat had already been roasted over the fire and the table was ready in the shelter. Everyone gathered around to eat, but I had no appetite and didn't feel well. I excused myself and found a grassy spot to lie down on a short distance from the shelter.

"Is he really sick?" I heard Haso ask from inside.

"No, something else is bothering him," said Sako.

Sako soon came out of the shelter and approached with two large goblets of wine and singing a beautiful song. His song was readily picked up and continued in hearty unison by those inside the shelter.

Hearing the emotion and innocence of these young voices rising up in the stillness of night from a ploughman's solitary shelter, I was overcome with the holy, vivifying power of social love. My heart filled with a sacred peace and the tempest that had so powerfully buffeted me came to an end at last. I could hold my tears back no longer and reached out for the goblet that Sako offered. We joined the circle of those who stood around the table with goblets in their hands. Garo delivered a little speech in grave and measured tones. But what he had to say that day came out of his mouth with such power and impact I will never forget, though that was fifty – yes, fifty! – years ago.

"My friends, we are the sons of a people who have been driven from their native land and dispersed to the four corners of the earth, whose hearths have gone cold for lack of fuel to burn, whose homes go dark after sunset because they have no oil for their lamps. We are the sons of a people whose children are forced to live without decent clothes; who go about in the scorching sun, the freezing cold and the drenching rain dressed only in tatters; who are sent to bed on empty stomachs because there isn't enough food for them to eat.

"And yet, we are not talking about a lazy or idle people. No, we are talking about a people who are constantly at work, who in fact work more than is humanly possible. Even women, girls, tiny children pitch in to help their fathers in their continuous labor. You know for yourselves how the women go out and bring the harvest back piled high on their heads and then thresh it with their own hands. You yourselves know how little girls go out into the fields to clear the weeds before planting. You have seen the little children riding on the yokes of oxen to help their fathers guide them.

"No, they are never idle for a moment. Yet, despite their year-round toil they remain mired in poverty, a bitter and unbearable poverty. And why? Because the land they live on, land that once belonged to their forefathers, has been taken over by foreign landlords. The land they work belongs to foreigners. The terms of their labor are crushing and pitiless and most of what they earn goes into their landlords' pockets and leaves them with hardly anything to live on.

"Every other aspect of the peasant's life is like that: His cottage sits on the landlord's land, and for that he has to pay rent. His animals graze on the landlord's land, and he has to pay a levy for that, too. The peasant and his family live, move, and have their being on the landlord's land. But to drink his water and be protected in life and limb he likewise has to pay a tax.

"In one word, the peasant owns nothing but his own laboring hands, and all of nature around him belongs to the landlord. So my friends, you see why our people are forced to emigrate and keep on doing so. They're forced to seek better fortune in foreign lands, because they can't sustain themselves in their native land. But do they ever come back? No, you know for yourselves how many hundreds of families have been left without the heads of their households, how many thousands of hearth fires gave gone cold because their men have gone off into exile.

"All of us gathered around this table come from homes exactly like that. We have no fathers, mothers or relatives. All of them have vanished from our lives. Therefore we can understand better than anyone what the laborers here have to bear, because we've experienced all those ills from birth; because each of us bears in his heart the incurable wounds of violent expropriation.

"We didn't receive the kind of ideas from our families that would have led us to challenge the landlord's cruel domination and throw off his yoke. They didn't prepare us to deal with the inevitable realities of life and to work only for ourselves. They didn't teach us how to keep an outsider from ripping the fruits of our labor out of our hands, because they were so completely downtrodden they accepted their oppression as part of the natural order. They didn't lift a finger in protest, because they considered their predicament ordained by God and believed there was no choice but to sacrifice themselves before an unalterable fate.

"The school we all attended further ingrained that submissiveness in us and destroyed our spontaneous energies. Father Todik inculcated blind obedience in us, the inclination to humble ourselves before anyone no matter how heavy the yoke they hung around our necks; that was the essence of how he related to us. He taught us that this worldly life is vain and transient, that the more painful and tormenting it is the greater our reward in the next life would be.

"But thankfully salvation came to us from a certain quarter and liberated us at last from the moral and mental decay that held us captive in school, and that beneficent hand set us on the right road. We were shown what it takes to attain a safe and secure existence in this life. We were taught how to help those downtrodden like ourselves find a better life, and we consecrated ourselves to improving the lot of the people.

"Brothers, let's drink to *that man* who inspired us to our task. Let's drink to the success of our mission and our sacred oath."

Once again the same vow, I thought as I listened, the same vow to save the impoverished peasants that was part of his dreams twelve years before.

The dreams that Garo and his cohorts shared seemed to me at that time not only unrealizable, but empty fantasies, the ravings of a sickly imagination. Was it truly possible to find relief for the peasants and free them from the clutches of the landlords, a class of men so powerful and enjoying such complete official sanction? How would it be possible to safeguard their livelihood when not one law had ever been passed to limit the landlords' whims; when even the central government's edicts were powerless to place a check on them?

I knew of thousands of cases in which edicts aimed at improving the lot of the people remained dead letters – for the khans and begs would force the messengers delivering them from the Sublime Porte to chew them up and swallow them on the spot, or force them to rip them to shreds, after which they would be beaten and placed on the road with the words, "Off with you now, and tell your king what happened to you." And thus these monsters were never punished; they never bowed to any authority and went on sucking the blood of the people.

Surrounded by his self-sacrificing comrades, Garo was carried away with powerful emotions. All of them were involved in trying to overturn an old order, struggling to shatter the chains of servitude that had been forged over so many centuries. But how?

Garo had very correctly observed that servitude had become second nature to the people. So what good could it do that a handful of individuals had awakened and understood what the people really needed, since all their efforts could simply be swallowed up and nullified in the face of the prevailing indifference? Their voices could be nothing but a cry in the wilderness. Their actions could only be condemned to the fruitless reconciliation of the grave. Garo was painfully aware of that. He knew that the masses were trapped in a kind of lunacy or drunkenness. He knew that they fell right down in the mud but didn't know how soiled they were; that they knocked their heads against the wall until they were bloodied but didn't feel any pain; that children passing by in the street would kick them and spit on them, yet they'd forget it and lie down meekly to sleep at night. Garo knew it all. He knew that the masses suffered economic torment, that they didn't have enough food to eat or decent clothes to wear but that they put up with their lot because they believed that suffering and disrespect were part of the established order, that none of it could be otherwise, and that the landlord could simply do whatever he wished.

So – how could you go about changing such deeply ingrained beliefs?

What could you do when the masses themselves did nothing to protest their intolerable predicament, when they patiently bore every misfortune, and – as Garo said in his speech – ascribed to such evils the status of laws predetermined from on high by God. What could you say to that?

Were these, indeed, the thoughts that ran through my head at the time? Not at all! These same misconceptions were part and parcel of my thinking at the time, too, for I was a typical child of that very same people.

I only laughed at Garo's fantasies at the time, just as I had twelve years earlier when he had fled Der Todik's school to join a very different kind of school and came under the influence of Hunter Avo, that remarkable man whose origins and homeland lay in mystery and whose true identity was hidden beneath the guise of a common hunter. But it was precisely this hunter of wild beasts who breathed a new spirit and a new consciousness into his fiery pupils . . .

Though the dinner concluded on an entirely happy note, I didn't feel any happiness at all. I was therefore very relieved when everyone decided to go to bed at last. But I couldn't fall asleep. Instead, I left the shelter and went out to wander for long hours in the dark of night.

The Great Festival of the Holy Mother of God

We arrived at the monastery on Saturday evening.

My first order of business was to set our tent up in a good spot so that we could all rest. Margarit and Khatoun were completely worn out from the journey and lay down to rest as soon as we arrived. Maro, too proud to show any sign of fatigue, helped me put up the tent and teased Margarit the whole time for being tired. I placed the tent in a central place, which is what Maro wanted, and it was ready to use in a quarter of an hour.

The monastery of the Holy Mother of God was located in the Gordvats Mountains near the shore of Lake Van and faced the Lim monastery island. Almost every monastery in Armenia has laid claim to some miraculous power or other and become famous for its special cures. The Holy Mother of the Gordvats region was known for healing skin diseases such as leprosy, rashes, and other lesions. However, not only did she offer hope to those who appealed to her for cures, she also inflicted those same afflictions on perfectly healthy people who disobeyed what the monks expected of them. For this reason leprosy, rashes, and certain types of wounds and canker sores were known as "the Mother of God's Wounds" and regarded as punishment for sins.

The Holy Mother of God of the Gordvats region was severe and vengeful. Her anger could be directed not only at people, but at animals as well. Such animals could not be used for work by their owners, whether cows, bulls, oxen, horses, or any other, because they bore the "marks" of the Holy Mother. The owners of such animals would either voluntarily turn them over to the monastery, or a 'pilgrim' representing the monastery would come and take them away. Every year these 'pilgrims' would go from village to village to gather these animals together. No Armenian had the right either to buy or sell them, as they were destined for the monastery.

Near the monastery was a village known as "Monastery Village." The villagers there were totally lazy and dull witted people who had no other occupation except serving the monastery. They were called "The Holy Mother's Pilgrims," and their livelihood depended exclusively on the monastery.

One couldn't help but be troubled to see the entire pitiful population of a village like that submit to serving the monastery and being blind tools in its hands. The Holy Mother's 'pilgrims' were uneducated folk but could quote entire chapters of the Gospel by heart. They knew the *sharagans*,[*] could recite proclamations of the church and, going from town to town, they enjoyed free access to any pious Armenian's home, whereupon they took out some sacred object, offered blessings, received reverent kisses from the inhabitants and left with alms.

These vagrants were everywhere. I still remember them coming into our house when I was a child and displaying some sacred object from the monastery, a cross or the relic of some saint. They would place the object on top of the sieve, then take hold of the sieve on all four sides while chanting various prayers. My mother would sit nearby while my sisters and I went underneath the sieve to receive the blessings that would fall through on us from the sacred object. After that the pilgrims performed the 'cleansing by the cross' and rubbed our faces with holy water and did a lot of other things that I've since forgotten. My mother was too poor to give them any money, but she never saw them off without giving them something of value – a gem out of her necklace or some bit of silver from her jewelry.

The monks handed out the sacred objects of the monastery to the pilgrims so that they could circulate them among the villages, but there were certain conditions attached. They would either rent them or sell them to the pilgrims with the understanding that a certain percentage of their earnings would come back to the monastery. But the pilgrims often took advantage of the people's superstition and reverence toward the monastery. Many of them used counterfeit crosses and 'holy objects.'

The Holy Mother's fame for the miraculous cure of skin ailments had reached every corner of the land, and the afflicted from near and far thronged to the monastery to be healed. In fact, many stayed on without any improvement at all in their condition and wasted their lives away there. Only now do I understand the dire results of the monks planting such superstition among the people. A good many of the diseases were

[*]. *Sharagans* or hymns.

communicable, and many of the infected pilgrims spread them among the general population. It wasn't rare for pilgrims who arrived at the monastery perfectly healthy to return home with a disease. These cases were only seen as the Holy Mother's punishment for certain sins.

Even the peasants in the monastery village became infected from their contact with the sick. Nowhere else could one find so many lepers and people with grotesque afflictions of the face and body as in the monastery village. Many crippling diseases became hereditary among them and were passed along from one generation to the next.

Moses prescribed special rules for dealing with lepers and others with communicable diseases. To this day such people are forced to live outside of communities. But the Holy Mother's pilgrims rejoice if their wives give birth to completely freakish children, because they see in them 'the marks of the Holy Mother.' The father of such a child can expect to gain handsomely from its condition. He will set the child on a donkey and parade it from place to place, inspiring awe toward the Holy Mother among the populace and raking in their money and gifts.

These victims of disease were called "The Holy Mother's Pitiful Ones."

Showing them off in public reinforced popular devotion to the monastery and increased the number of pilgrims. The monks had no objection at all to these fraudulent practices since they profited from them.

It has turned into a common curse among Armenians to say, "May you be struck with the mark of the Holy Mother." No one thinks without terror in their heart of the Holy Mother of the Gordvats mountains. She is a vengeful and hard-hearted saint.

At that stage in life I was as ignorant as everybody else and was under the sway of the same superstitions. But when I started to study Armenian history I discovered how intimately these traditions were connected with the era in which Nerses the Great established numerous monasteries as havens for lepers and cripples throughout Armenia. There they lived their lives and were cared for well apart from society at large. But with the passage of time these monasteries were subjected to the influence of popular superstition and lost their original purpose.

It was entirely dark now but none of the pilgrims had gone to sleep yet. The large expanse surrounding the monastery was filled with tents, and the colorful lanterns hanging in front of them created a magical atmosphere. There was one family in each tent. Some stayed outside beneath the open sky. Armenians from every country, from Asia to Persia, from the districts of Ararat, could be found in this helter-skelter mass of people. Most of them came from Aghbag, Van, Moush, and Bitlis.

I left my tent to go and look around in hopes of running into someone from Salmast. Maro wanted to go with me. Margarit and Khatoun were too tired to move. . . Maro and I wandered through the tents for a long time. Everything was abustle. People were jostling and crowding in on each other. The air was filled with song, murmurs, laughter, curses, prayers; and sometimes tender words from the lips of the young . . .

New doctrines can never completely supplant the notions a people have inherited from earlier days. In the course of the centuries pagan rites and forms of worship have struck deep root in the Armenian soul and become a lasting part of its nature. Christianity couldn't purge Armenia of its ancient ways until time and culture could infuse them with a new character.

As we walked through the tents some new sight came into view with every step we took. Maro was quiet and only rarely spoke a word. She ran from one scene to another like a butterfly flitting from one flower to another but seemed to find nothing to really hold her interest and soon became bored with it all.

In one spot an ashough was holding forth with a saz. With the instrument tucked against his breast, he played, sang, and recited an ancient tale surrounded by an appreciative crowd. His audience listened with rapt attention, encouraging him with donations and shouts of praise.

In another place two ashoughs were holding forth vigorously, locked in gladiatorial combat with each other in a contest of musical craft and intellectual agility. One posed a question in song, the other had to reply instantaneously in kind, every measure and note matching that of his competitor. These extemporaneous exchanges took place at astonishing speeds, and if one of the musicians was slow to respond or failed to match his competitor's phrasing perfectly, he was defeated and had to relinquish his saz to the victor – this lyre conferred by the Muses being the winning poet's prize.

Elsewhere musicians were playing zournas and drums, standing on level ground and surrounded by festive crowds. The people began dancing the Halli or Zvand. All ages joined hands in a circle, the musicians in the center, the jagged circle moving around them. The women's faces are veiled, the girls' are open. A young man with a fluttering handkerchief in his hand takes the lead and breaks into song with the *Jangyuloum*,[*] and as he finishes each line, its final words are repeated by the chorus.

The singing sometimes takes the form of a competition between the men and the women in which they alternately trade witty remarks with each other.

The style or form of the dance is maintained by specific steps, and sometimes the circle takes twists and turns that render it a massive labyrinth, but one in which the dancers never get mixed up with each other.

"Shall we join in?" I asked Maro.

"No, let's go see what else we can find," she answered.

Pushing our way through the crowd, we went up to the top of the monastery grounds where a very different spectacle was taking place and Maro was stunned by what she saw:

A crowd was gathered around a young woman who was collapsed on the ground in the throes of a seizure. She was foaming at the mouth, her eyes were aflame with utter madness and her limbs were quaking. Her possessed behavior gave signs that she was being tormented by some invisible power. Muted, dark, incoherent words escaped her lips from time to time. She was referred to as "the fallen one."

A vartabed stood near her with a small cross in his hand. From the movements of his beard he seemed to be saying a prayer.

"The fallen one" lost consciousness again, her mind overwhelmed by some higher force. She remained still for several moments, then began emitting deep sighs, uttering shocking words and calling on the names of angels, demons, devils, and various saints.

The vartabed placed the small cross in "the fallen one's" mouth. She readily closed her mouth around it. A few moments later the vartabed took hold of the chain to which the cross was attached and pulled it out of her mouth.

---

[*]. *Jangyuloum* ("O Precious Rose" from Persian and Turkish). A divination song and dance in Armenia.

"The fallen one" came to her senses a little, but there was still a frightful look on her face and her eyes reflected a terrible inner disturbance.

The vartabed put the cross in her mouth again, repeating this action three more times. Having considerably regained consciousness, the "fallen one" began to make sounds:

"Vanetsi Shushan-Khatoun should come forth, the Holy Mother is calling for her."

Shushan-Khatoun was the wife of a rich merchant who had remained childless after more than ten years of marriage. She soon showed up on the edge of the crowd with an awestruck look on her face.

The fallen one now began muttering nonsense:

"Yelisabet gave a sign . . . Blind Maryam conceived . . . The child rejoiced in her womb . . . Who is it that loosens the seal of infertility . . . It's the Holy Mother . . . Let everyone praise her . . . Light is shed from above . . . Blessed are they who see it . . . Blessed are they that hear . . ."

The vartabed began to interpret what the girl was saying for Shushan-Khatoun. He told her that the Lord, meaning the Holy Mother, had heard her plea and undone the seal of her infertility. She would give birth to a child who must be dedicated to the monastery for the first seven years of its life and carry out the pilgrimage every year to bring blessings on Her afflicted ones during the great festival.

Shushan-Khatoun rejoiced and, throwing off the heavy chain from around her neck, prostrated herself before the fallen one.

The prophetess fell into her trance once more, her mouth foaming, her face showing signs of horror. She murmured as if talking to some invisible presence. The vartabed was manipulating the cross. The girl came to her senses a bit and called out:

"Call Mshetsi Krikor."

That gentleman stepped forward, and "the fallen one" delivered her sermon to him:

"An unfair payment is harsh . . . Black chickens, a red cat will be my payment . . . Why isn't your heart shaken . . . You take no harvest from a hidden place . . . Alak . . . Palak . . . Take it . . . Bring it . . . Rejoice . . ."

The vartabed explained her divination as follows:

"Rejoice" means it ended well, it ended happily.

Then a false smile appeared on his face, and he went on:

Alak, palak meant of many colors; that is to say silken cloth fringed with gold stitching, meaning the curtain in front of the sanctuary.

"The Lady demands something from you," said the monk to Mshetsi Krikor. "You'll henceforth be happy, and what you wanted will be granted to you. The Lady's sanctuary curtain is old."

Divinations followed one after the other. Noteworthy was the fact that The Lady, through her mouthpiece, was calling on the richest and best known pilgrims from every quarter, and they all listened with deep humility to their sentences.

Then the diviner fell into complete unconsciousness and was carried off by the vartabeds who indicated that she would remain in that state and kept in a cave until all the pilgrims had arrived for the festival.

"Poor thing!" said Maro. "How can she stay in such a place. She might die there. Farhad, I'd like her to tell me something too. Don't you believe in her?"

"I do," I answered.

And that was true at the time. But if Maro asked me now I'd tell her that in the days when mankind worshipped the three-legged goddess Beauteas, she communicated the same kind of messages to them. That, again, was an ancient custom that had survived from the pagan era of Armenian history.

We left ecclesiastical prophetics behind us and headed into the prophetics of the people.

A little girl was sitting on a high rock far away. Her narrow, delicate face was bathed in walnut oil and reflected the light of a torch that burned nearby. She wore a dress of a motley, magical style and was surrounded by a group of young girls. This little girl was also engaged in divination.

We approached.

"That's the girl," said Maro.

"That's Hyubri," I said.

Hyubri recognized us both.

"Come on and let me do a divination for you. I won't ask for any money," she said smiling. "When did you get here? Where's your mother?" I asked teasingly.

Before she could answer, Susann appeared, gave me a suspicious look, and muttered something to her. The little waif jumped down from the rock and the two of them disappeared into the dark of night.

"Why did they run off as soon as they saw us?" asked Maro.

"I don't know. The old sorceress always makes sure that Hyubri stays away from me," I answered. "Hyubri is a little a demon, that's for sure," said Maro.

A little girl standing near us spoke up:

"She claims that her mother stole her from her cradle in the house of some demons. That's the truth, too, otherwise how could a little child like her know everything the way she does. She told me everything that was in my heart and everything that I have done."

After we had left the crowd Maro said to me:

"Garo or one of his friends must be around here somewhere."

"What makes you think so?"

"That sorceress and Hyubri are always behind him wherever he goes. Wherever Garo is, they are sure to show up."

"I don't understand. What would Garo and his friends have to do with those Gypsies?"

"I don't know myself," said Maro. "But I'll tell you one thing, Farhad, that little waif they call Hyubri speaks Armenian and she speaks it like an Armenian."

"Gypsies speak all kinds of languages."

"But this is different. One time I said to her, 'Hyubri, come and live with us at our house and be my sister.' She said, 'No, I'm going to join my mother, she loves me very much.' She said this in Armenian, but as soon as the old woman heard it she got mad at her and dragged her away."

"She's always looking for her mother, Maro. That's all she talks about, but I can't imagine how she'll find her."

"I know," said Maro.

On the way back to our tent we took the path that runs through the "Gorge of Trial." It is on this path that lies the "Boulder of Fate," a boulder so named because pilgrims tested their fate on it by picking up a small stone at its base and placing it on the boulder to see if it stayed where it was put or fell down. If the stone stayed in place, this meant their wishes would come true, but if it fell it meant bad luck and they would walk away from the mystic boulder sadly. Maro ran toward the boulder to try her luck but the crowd was too large for her to find a spot, so we left that for another time.

Van

On reaching Van, Aslan and I took up lodging in the suburb called Aykesdan[*] in the home of a gentleman named Varbed Panos, a dyer by trade and one of the notables of the district.

My first impression of him was of an upright and decent gentleman, a man with a firm build and a cheerful disposition. In the East a good physique is often the basis for a man's success in life. But beyond that Varbed Panos had a way with words and seemed an intellligent and well-traveled man. This was why, despite his relative youth, he had been elected a member of the local council, an organization in which advanced age and grey whiskers usually carry more weight than sound thinking.

It was completely dark by the time we reached his house.

Aslan now began relating to me more 'man to man,' as they say. As soon as we went in he introduced me to Varbed Panos, explaining that I had been one of his best friends in childhood and now his main comrade. Varbed Panos took stock of me from head to foot with a penetrating look, then very cordially said how pleased he was to meet me. Evidently he had known Aslan for a long time and had been expecting him. He also knew where we had just been. After we had settled down a bit he began questioning us very seriously:

"Why did your pilgrimage take so long?"

"That's just the way it turned out," said Aslan with equal gravity. "I hope the Holy Mother fulfilled all your wishes. . ."

"She'd never see her pilgrims off without conferring her blessings. . ."

"Wonderful! That calls for a glass of brandy to toast your success," said Varbed Panos, twisting the right tip of his moustache with delight.

"Not a bad idea, but we need a little something to eat first, we're famished," said Aslan.

"Well, that's quite understandable," said Varbed Panos with a smile. He rose to go out and call for some food to be brought.

---

*. Aykesdan was the verdant agricultural suburb of Van where most of the Armenians lived by the end of the 19th century.

Aslan settled down on a cushion and lay gazing up at the dark ceiling beams while lost in thought. I had some thinking to do, as well. Though it's laughable, I have to admit that one of my main wishes on coming to Van was to see one of its famous cats. Wasn't there just one cat in all that house? I wondered and looked around impatiently. Sometimes mysterious coincidences happen. A person will be thinking about something one moment and in the next it appears. Just at that moment in came my little beauty with a completely dramatic aura, as white as snow, with long, delicate fur and with paws as soft as velvet. It passed through the room silently and came up to me first, softly rubbing its curly head and thick furry tail across my face, then went over to say hello to Aslan. It circled around him a few times, all the while purring graciously, then sat down beside him. This intelligent animal apparently knew which of us deserved the most attention. Aslan petted its lovely head, its back and its tail and the more he petted it the more its thick fur crackled and gave off a cloud of sparks, a phenomenon I had never seen before.

"What's that?" I asked.

"Sparks," said Aslan, explaining to me the natural causes of this effect and how rubbing produces it.

Besides the cat no other members of the household had appeared. The children must have been in bed, for there was no sound from them, and the women in this part of the country would never present themselves before men.

Aykesdan lived up to its name. This lovely suburb is a vast area of lush vineyards and orchards divided by wide roads which are bordered on both sides by brooks running through the shade of willow trees. The houses are hidden from view and have no windows facing the roads, the only opening toward the roads being their main gates. The back of the houses face nothing but their gardens, and the life of each house is centered within itself, making for complete privacy. The same was true of Varbed Panos's house. We were given a room in the upper story of his house, a very comfortable room, apparently reserved just for guests. All the most beautiful things in the house were placed there to decorate it. Numerous kinds of plates were set near the windows, both of rustic and of Persian style and so old that they were no longer used. There were bronze cups, candleholders, large round trays all finely embossed with designs. There were also several long-stemmed nargilehs and chipouks made of jasmine or cherry wood from Shiraz. The large assortment of nargilehs and *chipuks*[*] testified to the visits of a great number of guests on occasion.

Singing could be heard coming from several rooftops, religious songs for the most part. The people here didn't have any secular songs, and the ones they sang were sad and doleful, the direct expression of the despairing self-denial through which people seek refuge in the spiritual and heavenly world when they are deprived of happiness in this one. Here and there people were strumming *chonkurs*,[†] their songs echoing in the silence of the night like the murmurs of a grieving heart. The song at a Vanetsi's table is, indeed, laced with tears.

I listened for a long time. The nocturnal silence was occasionally broken by jumbled moans, a disturbance that became increasingly hard to ignore. Then there was a gun shot, after which perfect silence reigned again. . .

"They're going berserk again! We'll find somebody dead or wounded in the morning," said Varbed Panos, rushing past me.

So – in one place killing, and in another religious song. But Varbed Panos was obviously not the sort to content himself with prayer. He came into the room, placed a glass of brandy and a tray of roasted *darekh*[‡] in front of Aslan, then grabbed one the guns off the wall and rushed away.

"Where are you going?" asked Aslan.

"There's a disturbance nearby. I have to see what's going on." Then, as if suddenly remembering something, he stopped short in the doorway. "A letter arrived for you today," he said, reaching into his breast pocket to pull out a thick packet which he handed to Aslan. He then rushed down the stairs.

Aslan held the letters up near the lamp and began reading them with close attention. I was sitting at some distance and following the succession of expressions on his face. His heart was in turmoil, and his gentle, peaceful eyes now flashed with anger. He was typically cautious in everything he did, but now seemed to forget that I was there. He took one of the letters and, half-read, flung it down to the floor and buried his face in his hands with despair. What had happened? Out of his trembling lips came only the same words, repeated over and over again, "Poor fellow,

---

[*]. A *chipuk* [chee-pook] is a long-stemmed wooden pipe with clay bowl.

[†]. A *chonkur* is a type of lute.

[‡]. *Darekh* or pearl mullet is the name of a small fish that is native to Lake Van.

poor fellow." It would have taken some truly great tragedy to disturb Aslan to this extent. He then picked the letter up from the floor, and continued reading it. After that, he held it up over the lamp and within seconds it was reduced to ash.

He then began reading the other letters, and now his expression seemed a little calmer, but his brow remained furrowed. He sometimes put the letter down to jot something in his notebook and do some figuring on his fingers. But one thing really made an impression on me: When he rubbed a certain fluid over one of the letters, hitherto invisible light green lines became visible between the original lines. How had they been hidden? I didn't dare ask because he was still rather tense. After reading the letters, he burned all of them and only then turned his attention to the food and drink before him.

"Ah, the darekh of Van! How many families survive on nothing but this little fish!" he exclaimed as he began eating. "Don't you like it?"

I didn't have any appetite. I was in very sad shape from the fatigue of traveling. A long and peaceful sleep was all that offered me any refreshment. But that was of no concern to Aslan. That man of iron didn't know what rest was, but waited impatiently for Varbed Panos's return. He returned a short time later and hung his gun back on the wall. He paced back and forth, saying "Intolerable! Intolerable! How long can this go on? My patience has run out!"

"What did you find out?" asked Aslan, with a smile.

"By the time I got there it was all over. The Kurds had already done their dirty work. I've had it! How long can this go on?" he responded.

Aslan's modest smile turned into laughter.

"Patience is life, that's what our forefather's taught us," he said sarcastically.

"Yes, but there's a limit to patience. Our patience is nothing but the silence of the grave."

"Describe what you saw," said Aslan.

"It was something too common, something that happens here every day, every night," said Varbed Panos, sitting down beside Aslan. "They were stealing fruit from the farms. When the Turks or Kurds come here to sell things, they're in the habit of stealing from Armenian farms when they leave in the evening. We're lucky if they only steal the fruit, but they totally destroy the trees when they do. You'll see them arrive all serious and quiet during the day. But as they pass by the farms they eye the trees and note which cherry or peach tree has wood they can use to repair their broken ploughs. At nightfall, they go into the orchards and cut those branches out. A tree it took the owner years to cultivate and develop is destroyed in one fell swoop, and the farm is left in a grotesque state. What suffering that is for the farmer! I've seen families sitting all day long with the broken branches of their trees, crying and wailing as if mourning the death of their own child."

Though this event had seemed so terrible to Varbed Panos, Aslan's reaction to it was very cool. It was nothing out of the ordinary in this province for a hardworking farmer to plant his trees, cultivate the soil, bring his crop to fruition, only to have it all taken away from him by a lazy, uncivilized people who used violence to take what they wanted.

"Wouldn't it be better if they made the robbers cry, rather than end up crying themselves?" said Aslan, interrupting Varbed Panos.

"Of course!" said Varbed Panos with a heavy sigh, "But that's a difficult proposition. They have brute power on their side. . . barbarity. Our hands are tied and theirs are free. . . We don't even have a stick to wield, yet they go everywhere they want armed with swords. We're defenseless. If a farmer shows the slightest resistance, if he doesn't allow his trees to be mutilated, I assure you that they'll come at night and slit his throat. And they will go unpunished, because around here an Armenian's head isn't worth a head of onion."

"But if they had weapons like those on your wall, then they wouldn't get their heads chopped off like so many onions," commented Aslan.

"Yes, if they had them!" said Varbed Panos heatedly. "But if an Armenian has a couple of ghouroush in his pocket all he thinks about is how to turn them into three, that's all he cares about. And that's how the government sees him. If they find him with a weapon in his hands they take it away and say, 'that's not for you, go and occupy yourself with commerce.' And so the Armenian remains a defenseless prey to the Kurd and Turk. They burn his harvest, they destroy his farm and all the Armenian does is stand there sighing and wringing his hands. . .'"

"Is the government really that unfair?" I asked.

"What government are you talking about? There's no such thing as a government here! There are only selfish functionaries who commit the same barbarities themselves."

The conversation went on and on. What good did it do to discuss such things, I thought. It's always the same talk, the same points:

One party is persecuted, the other is the persecutor. What can be done to alleviate the victim's suffering, and so on? You would think they were the apostles of the great Son of God, who said, "Come unto me all you who suffer and are heavy laden, and I will give you rest."

I became lost in thought – such a jumble of thoughts, so confused and disconnected that I could hardly make sense of them. One image after another came and went in my reverie, memories of the countless times and mysterious forms in which I had seen Aslan:

In the middle of a wilderness in an Arab minaret with his band of outlaws, waiting for night to fall and the traffic on the roads to stop; waiting for the world to go soundly asleep so that he and his cohorts could carry on their secret work.

I would sometimes see him in the garb of a monk, walking by with slow, measured steps, then disappearing into the forest. I would see him in the tent of a Yezidi chieftain, in the garb of a common Vanetsi merchant. And now, as the house guest of an eccentric Vanetsi, I saw him as a physician who held one of the highest degrees offered by European universities. But he had ordered me to keep his Armenian identity a strict secret. Why? Why did he shun his Armenian name and continually change his identity in different times and circumstances? Such were the thoughts that preoccupied my mind without leading to any clear answer.

But there was one thing about Aslan that stood out distinctly from everything else: From the first day we set out on our journey together, wherever we went, whatever the circumstances, the people whose company he sought out were always those who protested the prevailing anarchy of the land. And it seemed some common thread ran through all of them and bound all their hearts and wills together, people of different nationalities. But who held the other end of that thread? All of them seemed to be individual parts of some grand, complex mechanism. But what force set it in motion and directed it, turning their many wills toward the same goal? To this day the answer has eluded me. As it seemed to me, it was the ruling spirit, invisible, unapproachable, but governing the hearts and minds of mankind with its powerful unseen hand and giving them all direction. . .

The Governor Pasha of Van

One morning Aslan told me he had an appointment to go into the city to meet the governor pasha of Van and wanted to take me with him. I was very happy at the prospect because I had never seen a high official before.

The pasha lived in the fortress of Van. Even though the city wasn't a great distance from Aykesdan, he sent horses for us to ride and two servants to lead us there. The horses came decked out in the most elaborate Asiatic style, a very special honor shown to the new guest, especially since it was normally forbidden for Christians to enter town mounted on horses.

The city lay close to the shores of Lake Van and the sight of it had a positively bewitching effect on me, perhaps because it was the largest human settlement I had ever seen. It was entirely surrounded by double walls fortified with pyramidal turrets and accompanied by deep moats. Aslan explained that in times of siege the moats were filled with water and the bridges raised to keep the enemy out. In addition to these external defenses, the town possessed the marvel of a citadel formed by nature itself. On the northern side of the town was a rocky crag that ran for more than a mile and, as it rose gradually higher and higher, culminated in a wedge-shaped summit. That summit had been magnificently occupied from time immemorial by a splendid fortress. Armenian legendary tradition attributed that fortress to the Assyrian queen, Semiramis.

But on passing through the main gate, I felt a thrill of anticipation mixed with a shudder of fear. The whole town seemed to be roiling like a gigantic anthill with the hubbub of some nebulous excitement. There were multitudes of people and animals everywhere. Large packs of dogs roamed free on all sides and there was barely any room to move forward. Our escorts had to force a path for us, and we were engulfed the whole time in a sea of resentful, hostile faces. It clearly didn't sit well with the Muslim throngs to see us 'infidels' cutting a more or less distinguished figure in public, with Aslan projecting the demeanor of a European consul or ambassador. As for myself that day, in keeping with Aslan's instructions I carried the full complement of my weapons: two pistols lashed to my saddle, two more stuck in my waistband, a light European rifle slung over my shoulder, and my sword with its eye-catching silver embellishments. The Armenians in the crowd were no better disposed toward us. Far from taking any pleasure in our status, they were only fearful lest the resentment of the Muslims be somehow provoked. They kept their heads down in their little stalls and remained totally engrossed in their business.

We finally arrived at the pasha's residence. It was quite unimpressive on the outside. On the inside, however, it breathed of every extravagance of an oriental despot: dancing water fountains, peacocks crying and strutting through flower beds, servants everywhere. We were received at the main gate by a high-ranking official who led us through a series of courtyards, each more striking than the previous one.

This residence full of greenery and opulence; this palace in which it had become a custom to spend whole nights in song and dance; where the foremost beauties of the land, flaunting their jewels, lounged about in silks and satins until the break of day; this paradise of love was at the same time a hell of tears and terror, for in the subterranean depths beneath its polished floors lay a labyrinth of dungeons echoing with the bitter moans and clanking chains of hundreds of prisoners. Its verdant courtyards and marble walkways had more than a few times been stained with the blood of innocents and its leafy trees more than once used to hang men. All of that transpired in moonlight beneath the shadowy ramparts of the fortress, with the still waters of the ponds reflecting the shocking crimes that took place there but were never heard of by the outside world.

I had been taught since childhood to be terrified of great men and quake in their presence. That's why waiting to see the pasha filled me with panic. Aslan, noticing the state I was in, reprimanded me and reassured me at the same time:

"You're still stuck in a slave mentality. Why are you so flustered? Isn't he just a man like you and not some mighty god?" I came to myself a bit, but more out of shame than encouragement.

The pasha received us with great courtesy. He looked to me like an enormous mound of flesh, if one can put it that way. He had a thick head, a broad belly, and coarse voice. In short, there was nothing subtle or refined about him at all, unless it was the intrinsic canniness of a high Turkish official, with all the cunning and deceit that entails. His attendants took him by the arms on either side and lifted him to his feet to greet us. Taking a few steps forward, he offered Aslan his hand.

"Doctor, there's no way for me to express how truly fortunate I feel that my home has been found worthy of a visit from such a distinguished guest as you," he said, continuing to hold Aslan's hand until he had sat him down on his right side.

His words were so flowing and pleasant you would think he had just rehearsed them the week before. But, no, it wasn't only the previous week that he had honed such fine phrases but rather in the course of his entire life, for he had long ago mastered the art of presenting a kind and courteous face to foreigners. With his own, however, it was another matter.

"Did you have a peaceful journey, doctor? I sincerely hope you had no problems."

"I can't complain. I was given a friendly reception wherever I went," answered Aslan.

"That's as it should be, doctor. I would have been very upset if you had run into the least problem in my territory. Europeans often take a dim view of our country and think of it as so lawless that people get their heads chopped off just for the hair to be found on them. So we very much welcome European visitors who can help dispel such unpleasant ideas."

"Actually, some European travelers have expressed a very high opinion of your country," observed Aslan.

"That's only as it should be, doctor. That will encourage more contacts between us, which will help our culture develop more and more. It's true we've had some disturbances here and there. But, after all, what country is entirely free of such things? Most of them happened in the previous period. If I say so myself – and you can ask what others think – I assure you that from the day I took office the wolf and the lamb have been getting along like true brothers."

"I can vouch for that myself," said Aslan cordially.

At this point a well-dressed attendant came in to serve coffee. In one hand he carried a silver tray with two extraordinarily beautiful china cups set in silver bases and in the other a pan of coffee. As was the custom, he filled the first cup and handed it to the pasha, who in turn passed it to his guest. Aslan thanked him graciously. The attendant then filled the other cup for the pasha.

As the attendant exited the room he brushed close by me and gave me a soft nudge with his elbow as a signal for me to leave with him and take my coffee apart. But to his amazement, I ignored him and stayed put.

When coffee was finished another attendant, dressed even more elegantly than the first, came in with a strikingly beautiful, gem-studded nargileh. Its burning bowl was of pure gold and its serpentine hose was fitted with an amber mouthpiece. The water bowl was made of gleaming crystal adorned with multicolored flowers. As he had done with the coffee, the pasha first took the nargileh from his attendant and then offered it to Aslan.

"You seem quite familiar with our customs here," observed the pasha with a laugh. "Do you like to smoke a nargileh?"

"Yes, I was introduced to it in Stamboul."

"But what were we just talking about?" asked the pasha.

"You were saying that the wolf and the lamb were getting along."

"Oh yes! I have so many things on my mind. Forgive me for running on so much, doctor. Europe slanders us in accusing us of treating our Christians poorly, alleging that we persecute them and subject them to every evil under the sun. Make no mistake, the Christians are better off here than the Muslims; they enjoy all sorts of advantages. We have spared them many obligations we expect only of the Muslims; military conscription, for instance, which they find so onerous. I have personally taken steps to improve their lot, to lighten their burden and safeguard their livelihood. And I'm happy to say that the Christians, for their part, haven't failed to appreciate my efforts. I'm grateful that not a month goes by without them showing their gratitude for all to see. Right now, doctor, I have a new public declaration to show you. It was made in two copies, one to be sent to the Armenian patriarchate of Constantinople and the other to the Sublime Porte. In them the Armenian populace, with thousands of signatures, expressed its deep appreciation for my government and called attention to its fortunate circumstances and well-being under my administration."

He ordered the servant who was stationed nearby to bring him his portfolio. He pulled out several pages covered with various seals and signatures, the most prominent of which was the seal of the Armenian patriarch, followed by the signatures of various Armenian begs, effendis, and other notables.

These papers made no small impression on Aslan and me. But when we returned to Aykesdan, Varbed Panos explained the shady sources of these congratulations.

Convinced that his display had achieved the desired effect, the pasha continued:

"In this enlightened century, we'd feel very ashamed if Europe saw us discriminating against Christians only because of their religion. It's true that our populace still hasn't rid itself of many age-old prejudices and remains quite intolerant. But where are such things unknown? The Jews still face persecution even in certain parts of Europe. Our government is doing all it can to reduce intolerance and educate the people. More schools are being built every day. We are even promoting the development of Armenian schools. There's a well known Armenian school in Aykesdan which I sponsor myself."

The dialogue was interrupted again, this time by an attendant bringing in a silver tray covered with a rich assortment of desserts.

"Try one of these *pakhlava*s,[*] doctor. The Armenian prelate loves them. He absolutely has to have some on his visits or he goes away very disappointed," said the pasha.

"He's entirely right, it's very well made," said Aslan.

"Have you met the prelate yet?" the pasha asked.

"No, I haven't had the chance yet."

"Well, you have to visit him, you owe it to yourself. An outstanding gentleman, the very best. Coming to Van and not seeing him is like going to Rome and not seeing the Pope."

"I'll take your advice, then. I won't leave town without seeing him."

The cordial relations between the Armenian prelate and the pasha were no secret to us. It was obvious why Aslan was being exhorted to visit the 'most honorable gentleman.' The pasha had every reason to expect the prelate to bear the same witness about him and refer to him likewise as that 'most honorable man,' and that glowing entries about these two high representatives of the country would eventually grace the travel notes of a European doctor.

The pasha gave himself away:

"He's my good friend and my eager partner in everything I do. I'm completely enamored of European culture, doctor. If I had the gift of miracles I'd turn our country into France in the twinkling of an eye. But that's impossible, unfortunately. We still have a lot of work to do. It will take leaps for us to catch up with the enlightened nations."

---

[*]. *Pakhlava* – a very sweet, flaky pastry topped with chopped nuts and syrup.

A slight smile played over Aslan's face:

"The normal education of a people doesn't require leaps," said Aslan. "They should be left to themselves to find their way naturally. The key is that they find the right road and not stray from it."

"There's a great deal of truth in what you say," the pasha responded with the air of an expert. "But our problem is that, with rare exceptions, our most important men are unscrupulous. How many times have I proposed to the grand vizier that a portion of the taxes be set aside for local improvements! But I've only been rebuffed. Thousands of things need to be fixed. For example, you've seen the sorry condition of our roads and bridges and canals. They all need repair. If we want to understand why our commerce and agriculture have collapsed, we have to look at our communications for the real causes."

Turkish officials have a gift for hatching plans but fall short in their execution. Give them money for their projects and it will go straight into their pockets. To Europeans, they typically present themselves as broadminded advocates of education and progress. But, after making a great show of their concern for the common people, they will throw up their hands in helplessness when confronted with the slightest unforeseen obstacles to their professed good intentions.

Having summoned all the diplomatic skill at his command up to this point, the pasha now shifted to ordinary conversation, turning to the sorts of things one usually discusses with one's doctor: stomach aches; loss of appetite; insomnia; foot pain, and some imaginary illness that he had difficulty explaining or was ashamed to speak about openly.

At last, he said:

"I want to be young again, doctor, make me young again. They say that European doctors know of a medicine that can turn a man young again."

"In what way?" asked Aslan, with a smile.

"It turns white hair black again. It changes a decrepit old man into a robust seventeen year old."

"Well, there is dye for turning the hair black, but a medicine that turns an old man into a youth hasn't been discovered in Europe yet."

"You mean to say there's no medicine that can give one a little more power, a little more strength?" the pasha asked. Thus, despite his cultural pretenses and high government office, he was asking his guest for one of those elixirs that the dervishes use to bewitch their leaders.

"I was told your son isn't feeling well," said Aslan, politely ignoring the pasha's request. "Please let me see him."

"No, don't bother yourself. He's not so sick he can't come on his own," said the pasha, apparently reluctant to allow the doctor into the women's quarters where the young man was being kept.

Within a few minutes a maidservant led a frail but quite beautiful boy of ten into the room, holding him by the hand. He was dressed from head to foot in a dark pink Ottoman suit decorated with beautiful designs. The child suffered from periodic fevers. Aslan examined him, gave him some medical advice, and promised to send some medicines for him.

In the course of that lengthy conversation I was impressed at how skillfully Aslan drew the pasha out without saying much himself. So charming was his demeanor, it seemed the pasha fell in love with him. And indeed, the pasha made it clear that he would be more than glad to see a great deal of Aslan, that his home had every convenience he needed and that, if he wished, he could stay there for the remainder of his visit to Van. Aslan declined his offer with gratitude, indicating that he simply could not take advantage of his lordship's unforgettable graciousness and that he only planned to stay in town a few more days. But he promised until then to visit the pasha and his son as often as possible and provide them with the medical attention they needed.

"Why are you in such a hurry, doctor?"

"Because I have to be in India exactly two months from now and I don't have time to spare. The only reason I am here is to see a few antiquities. My next stop is Mosul. I want to see the ruins of ancient Nineveh. From there I'll go through Baghdad to see Babylon, and then I'll sail for India."

"We have quite a few antiquities here that haven't been examined yet," said the pasha. "You made the right decision to include us in your itinerary."

"I'm especially interested in the wealth of cuneiform inscriptions you have here in Van."

"Yes, we have a real wealth of them! I'll give you a guide who can take you wherever you want and show you everything. He'll take you to the citadel where you'll find many of those inscriptions you're interested in."

That was Aslan's exact purpose in bringing up the cuneiform inscriptions: to see the citadel. So, expressing great thanks, he stood up.

The pasha stood up too and accompanied him to the door to see him off, showering his 'precious guest' with flattery the whole time.

When our visit with the governor was over, his servants escorted us back to Aykesdan in the same manner as they had brought us and delivered us right to Varbed Panos's door. As soon as we were inside Aslan threw his hat off with a laugh and shook his head in amazement.

"Clever people, so very clever!" he exclaimed. "They really know their game. If I were really a European and didn't know any better, I'd be totally taken in by the scoundrels."

Varbed Panos came in at that point and asked Aslan how his visit to the governor had gone. Aslan gave him a quick sketch, then added the following:

"If you knew European languages and could read what European travelers write about Turkish people and officials, you'd think they were completely out of their minds. They describe the Turks as a good-natured, industrious people, with a penchant for progress. They find Turkish dignitaries high-minded and magnanimous. In short, they are completely taken in by the Turks and can't find enough good things to say about them. How does such a thing happen? Imagine for yourself some European nobody who is treated with complete contempt even by lowly servants in his home country but suddenly gets it into his head to travel to the East. Simply being a European and coming from one of Europe's famous cities is enough to assure him a good reception wherever he goes. Furthermore, ambassadors and consuls supply him with all the letters of recommendation he needs to help him along in his travels. If he runs into poor treatment anywhere, his country's representatives immediately know how to apply pressure where it is needed to protect him. In his home country he would be kept waiting for hours in an ante-room to see an important official. But in Asia the doors of the highest officials are flung open to him simply because he's a European and has it in his power to give them a good or bad name. He's totally oblivious of the many crimes they have committed and, because they are on their best behavior, he assumes the best about them.

Everything he learns about the country's economic and social conditions comes from them, and by the time he sits down at a desk to write his travel notes he is still under the sway of their overwhelming hospitality. And what an extravagant desk it turns out to be! Never in his life has he been near anything like it! Intoxicated with sheer delight, he then sits down to write all the misinformation he has been fed by his hosts, imparting to his observations the same pleasure he felt while downing the fragrant sherbets and delectable pastries he was just offered. If his false accounts make it into the European press they will have a wide impact and mislead the public, since they are based only on superficial and fascinating appearances, rather than on penetrating, well-founded observation. What else can come of such a traveler's superficial glances around him, especially when his guides are pashas and their like? If one seriously wants to investigate the state of a people, one has to go to the people themselves, not to their rulers.

Brother Teos's Coffeehouse

The coffeehouses of Van usually open at sunrise and close at sundown, at which point every sign of life, every movement, comes to a stop. Those who don't wish to gamble on the whims of the police choose to stay indoors, as only thieves and their counterparts, the night watchmen, are abroad at those hours. At any other time of year the coffeehouse we were looking for would have been closed, but it was the month of Ramadan. During this month, day is turned into night and night into day for the Muslims. All day they fast and sleep, and at night they wake up to eat and pray together. Many of the bakeries, jewelry shops, and grocery stores were still open as we entered the town. The only lighting in the streets came from such establishments. People were still going up and down the streets, some on their way to mosques, some on their way to join neighbors for a night of feasting and religious observances. Rich people had invited their poorer neighbors to dinner. For one entire month out of the year, the Muslim became contrite and pious.

Aslan seemed familiar with brother Teos's coffeehouse and found his way straight there without asking directions. When we arrived he immediately went to a little door in the back of the building and knocked. A servant promptly opened the door, and we went in.

"Can I see brother Teos?" Aslan asked.

"He's in the coffeehouse," the servant answered.

"Go get him. Tell him there's a gentleman here who has some business with him."

"And your name?"

"You don't need my name. Just have him come here."

The servant walked off muttering to himself. We waited in the small yard. Within a few moments brother Teos appeared with a lantern in his hand. He gave Aslan's face a searching look, then after several moments said:

"Please come in."

He led us into a tidy room, furnished in a half-Eastern and half-European style and set the lantern on a small round table in the center.

"Now, what did you want?" he asked in the tone of an innkeeper seeking to please his guests.

"Something to drink," said Aslan.

Brother Teos left and soon came back carrying two bottles of wine over which he had placed inverted cups like caps. Placing them on the table, he said:

"This wine comes all the way from Bitlis, and now I've got only one bottle of it left, but I swear – even if my own father returned from the grave and asked for some, I wouldn't give it to him! It's just for me."

"All the best stuff you keep to yourself, isn't that so, Brother Teos?" Aslan said with a laugh.

"Well, what is a man to do? The Prophet prays for his own needs first," he responded with the well-known Turkish adage. He then held each cup up to the lantern to make sure it was clean. Not satisfied, he took the towel off his shoulder and gave them another polishing.

There was a certain familiarity in the way Brother Teos related to Aslan, although, to be sure, a coffeehouse proprietor was always as polite with his customers as a parson with his pious flock.

Aslan poured the wine, and it turned out to be even better than Brother Teos had indicated. Seeing how pleased we were, he set some cured meat on the table, urging us to have it with the wine to enhance our enjoyment.

Brother Teos was a diminutive man, with a sad, bleak expression, but sharp and lively eyes. A bit of a pot belly didn't detract much from a well-built frame, but his head was sunken back on his shoulders. Like many Vanetsis, he had gone to Bolis in his youth to try his luck (There is hardly a Vanetsi who's never made several trips to Bolis as a young man). Brother Teos had tried his hand at several jobs, but none of them had worked out.

If he had been endowed with a sturdy frame he might have become a hamal, a stoker on a ship, a stevedore, or a butler in a rich man's house. To be a butler one also had to be stately and have a fine face, which Brother Teos didn't. So the only job he could find was as an assistant to the coffee brewer in a coffeehouse. With this job he was barely able to earn enough money to cover his return trip to his native city; but though he returned with an empty wallet, he had learned a great deal from his difficulties in exile and was chastened by all he had seen and learned, including things he eschewed and found unworthy to bring back to his homeland . . .

Brother Teos didn't stay with us for very long, but ran off to take care of another customer. Just at that moment, a door opened into the room, and a little child rushed in. Seeing us, the child stopped a few feet away and stood staring at us for several moments, then ran out of the room again crying, "I'm well now, doctor. I don't need you anymore."

This was enough for me to see that Aslan was no stranger to this house.

"The child knows who you are," I said to him.

"No matter, he's too smart to betray me," he said, at the same time looking around as if expecting someone.

I left Aslan in the room to visit the coffeehouse right next door. Brother Teos's home occupied the back of the building, and the front, which opened onto the street, was the coffeehouse. The coffeehouse was an enormous hall lit with oil lamps. The walls were lined with wooden benches for the customers to sit on cross-legged. Every kind of person could be seen here: merchants, shopkeepers, government officials, shiftless beggars, as well as completely idle drifters, all of them smoking nargilehs, drinking coffee, and playing backgammon or other games. The faces of this motley crowd could hardly be distinguished through the thick haze of smoke. I just sat down on one side and took in the sight of all these people. They had come here all worn out from a hard day's work and now, under the numbing influence of smoke and bitter coffee, surrendered themselves to a certain intoxication of self-forgetfulness.

This was one of the main coffeehouses of Van. Having spent long years in Bolis, brother Teos had introduced certain innovations from the great capital, but for the most part his establishment retained its provincial character. Everything was done right in front of the customer. The coffee was brewed right at the table and poured out from the long-handled coffee pan. These coffee pans came in a variety of sizes, some hardly bigger than a thimble, and they would be poured out into a cup of matching size. In this way no matter what the order, it could be easily accommodated.

But the orders kept coming: "A coffee!" some customer would call out. "With or without sugar?" the coffee brewer would ask, and as soon as the customer's desire was made clear, the brewer would put a few drops of water into the thimble – which is to say, the coffee pan – and hold it over the brazier for a few moments, then pour the coffee powder into it. With that the black liquid was ready and served to the customer, his bill being written on the wall in charcoal. Within a few hours, hundreds of names had covered the walls. And thus they all went on smoking their nargilehs and calling out when they wanted more coffee.

Brother Teos's coffeehouse served his customers' other needs, too:

Behold, in one corner of the room a talkative barber who had just finished shaving a Turkish man's head and face, bent over the customer to pluck the hairs out his ears with tweezers, and, to lighten his own labors, recounting to him the news of the day and the latest episodes from the lives of notable gentlemen.

While this was going on, the barber's assistant was engaged in a different activity, something cruder still. He was preparing to pull someone's tooth. The patient was kneeling in front of the barber's assistant like a condemned man, his head held back from behind by another man. A third man held down the patient's hands, while the barber's assistant approached like an executioner and stuck huge forceps into his mouth. With a few powerful pulls and muted groans from the patient the work was over, and the forceps emerged with two bloody teeth in its grip.

"Hurrah! Instead of one tooth, you got two!" sounded off the onlookers.

"Damn you! The bad tooth is still in my mouth!" the patient shouted, and everyone laughed.

Wherever I looked some new scene greeted my eyes: Over there, behold, some folk musicians sitting on the floor, playing their traditional instruments; further off, a fervent Muslim finishing his ritual ablutions, making use of the same little earthenware bowl that had been used for changing the water in the nargilehs. He rose up from his wooden seat now, and, kneeling, standing, and doing several prostrations, completed his prayers in front of everyone.

In another place everyone's attention was focused on a particular group of people known as *tiriyaki*s. They were quite conspicuous as they sat cross-legged in the furthest corners of the hall, and people watched them curiously to see what they would do. They seemed to be slumbering. Their heads hung down with the stems of nargilehs gripped in their teeth, and their eyes were half shut. Only the smoke escaping from their lips from time to time gave any evidence that these stupefied, immobile beings had any consciousness at all. They would leave their houses early in the morning to come to the coffeehouse to wash up, comb their hair, say their prayers, and purge themselves of the previous day's excesses.

The waiters at the coffeehouse were quite familiar with them all and entirely ready to help them in any way. These pathetic folk sat in the same place all day, prodding their brains with bitter coffee, tobacco smoke, and little doses of opium. Their faces bore idiotic expressions as they sat with glazed eyes and trembling hands.

Right next to these idiots the light of the Gospel was being spread by someone in the pay of missionaries, and he engaged onlookers in religious debate, an open bible in hand. A few curious people stood around him, listening, cursing, and arguing with him.

My attention settled on three men sitting far across the room at a round table with a bottle of brandy on it. One was a young man whose clothing was like that worn by the Armenians of Mosul or Baghdad.

He was wrapped in a long cloak with black and white stripes like those of pilgrims on the hejaz. The long tasseled fringes of his Arabic style turban fell down to his shoulders, and his forehead and eyes were barely visible beneath the colorful silk covering over his face which was tied at the top of his head. I immediately thought that this must be the merchant from Mosul whom Aslan had come to see. The two men with whom he was talking seemed stranger still on account of their worn looking, half-European and half-Asiatic clothing. It appeared they had spent a good deal of time traveling through those countries in which tight breeches and wide brimmed hats are worn. Now on their return to Asia only various portions of European clothing still clung to their bodies.

Pointing out the young Mosultsi to Brother Teos, I asked, "Who is that man?"

"That's khoja Toros, a tobacconist from Mosul," Brother Teos responded casually. "And what about those other two with him?"

"I don't recognize them. They're new to me."

With that, Brother Teos went off. I began looking more closely at the tobacconist. He had pulled away the Arabic face covering because of the overwhelming heat in the coffeehouse. His pallid looking face didn't conform with the usual sunburned look of people from Mesopotamia, and his darting eyes seemed very familiar. He was so involved in the conversation he was having that he didn't notice me at all, or, if he did, he tried not to show it. I went up behind him and gently placed my hand on his shoulder.

Looking back at me, he gave me a signal with quick movements of his eyes which left me confused and silent. Then he relieved my confusion by indicating a place for me to sit down.

"Please have a seat, sir. I can see that you're new to this town like us. Outsiders feel more comfortable in each other's company. There's still enough brandy left in our carafe for a few more glasses," he said, picking up the carafe and shaking it around as if to prove what he had said.

Who could have imagined that here in this jumble of humanity I would have found our old comrade Sako in the guise of a merchant called Toros khoja. How well the name suited him, as well as the Arabic clothing and that resonant, guttural voice as he spoke with such seriousness to the two strangers.

I had been so familiar with Sako's merry ways, his sharp sarcasm, and his nimble wit that all it took was for me to look at his face and I'd have to laugh despite myself. But now that I had even more to laugh about, given his outlandish appearance, I couldn't let myself, but just sat there speechless and amazed at my predicament.

He asked me a couple of questions about who I was, where I was from, what business had brought me to Van, then filled a glass with brandy and set it in front of me.

"I'm not used to brandy," I said.

"Then I'll order some wine for you," he said, calling a waiter.

He then introduced me to his guests at the table, two poor young men who seemed to be the agents of an equally poor, but morally rich, organization based in Bolis which had sent them to the environs of Kharpert, Sghert, and Dersim to teach Armenian to the Kurdish speaking Armenians there. Despite this modest and innocent purpose, the young men had found themselves vilified by Protestant preachers and persecuted by the government as so many troublemakers trying to infect the population with dangerous ideas. They had abandoned their mission and ended up in Van totally broke on their way back to Bolis.

Continuing the previous topic of discussion, one of the young men pointed to the preacher who was spreading the light of the Gospel for some foreign missionary and was pressing on with the religious debate, open bible in hand. "Look at him. I'll bet you anything that good-for-nothing has no education or culture. He's probably so bad at what he does that he only gets paid a hundred ghouroush (6 roubles) a month. Yet every day he goes into coffeehouses, barbershops, public squares – in a word, any place that people gather – and he engages them in debate. He doesn't have any convictions or beliefs of his own, and he argues whatever case he's paid for, like a lawyer. He doesn't have the least interest in anything that involves national ideals, history, the fatherland, or the tragic state of the people. These don't even exist for him. All he knows is that no one can be saved from sin by keeping fasts, confessing to priests, or worshiping pictures, and he opposes these practices as well as anything that resembles them. No matter where in Asia Minor you go you will find these babblers. And it goes without saying that their congregations, their schools, their preachers – those ignorant hundred-ghouroush-a-month disseminators of the light – are all cut from the same cloth."

Sako listened to all of this in total silence, and I found what the young man said equally as fascinating. It seemed the young man was not so bothered by the preaching of foreigners as by this blind, fanatic, gullible Armenian allowing himself to be used as a puppet in their hands.

"I'm no defender of religion or the national church," continued the young man. "And yet I'll say that people like him are more harmful to Armenians than Kurds or Turks. Turks and Kurds rob Armenians of the fruit of their labor. That's a loss that can be recouped through hard work. But these preachers – these spiritual predators – destroy national identity in the name of the Gospel, and that's an irrecoverable loss."

"How so?" asked Sako, filling his glass with wine and his companions' glasses with brandy.

The young man lit his small pipe and let some puffs of smoke escape his quivering cheeks covered with their first growth of facial hair. "Like this," he said. "Take the areas we were just working in and where we were harassed, for example. The Armenians there have lost their mother tongue. They only speak Kurdish. They've lost their distinctive national character, and they follow Kurdish ways. Their only tie with the rest of the nation is the Armenian church, and if that link is severed what is left to tie them to the rest of Armenians?"

"Nothing at all," said Sako, as if eager for the young man to get to his point.

"And so we can see the harm done by Protestant preachers, how they go about killing national consciousness," he went on heatedly. "Pullling Armenians from the bosom of their church, they're turning them into nothing but Protestant Kurds."

"What's surprising about that?" asked Sako, raising his head and looking directly into the young man's eyes. "You just said that the Armenians in those areas had lost their distinctive national character and are living according to Kurdish ways. If that's true, how can you justify calling them Armenians? Only because they belong to the Gregorian church? That's just the problem, and it's led us to the wrong conclusions. They stopped being Armenian from the day they stopped speaking Armenian. From that day on they became Gregorian Kurds. It's quite obvious that if they've forsaken the Gregorian church and become Protestants, they've turned into Protestant Kurds. And, further, if they then forsake Protestantism to become Buddhists, they become Kurdish Buddhists."

The two young men looked at each other in amazement, and Sako went on:

"The same thing happened with the Arabic speaking Armenians of southern Mesopotamia, Mosul, and Baghdad. They lost their mother tongue and followed Arab ways. They only considered themselves Armenian because they still belonged to the Gregorian church. Then Catholicism took hold among them, they stopped calling themselves Armenians and turned into Catholic Arabs. Some of them spoke the Chaldean language and became part of the Chaldean Catholics."[*]

This conversation went on for quite a while, since the topic was vital both to the young men and to Sako. The question of religious conversion had become a dominant issue for all Armenians. Foreign proselytizers, whether Catholic, Protestant, or Jesuit, had turned up everywhere among the Armenians and spread through countless towns and villages. They founded schools and assembly halls. The people were in a restive state and were abandoning the Armenian church. Some left for the money the preachers offered to new believers; some for the protection from the depredations of the Muslim populace the missionaries promised. Others were leaving out of disgust with the greed of the priests and monks; and others, very few in number, were leaving out of genuine conviction. The Armenian people were falling apart. There were perpetual quarrels, disturbances, and divisions everywhere.

---

[*]. Chaldeans are ethnic Assyrians whose church is in communion with the Catholic church.

In that state of affairs, it was impossible for any thinking person to ignore the awesome forces that threatened to shatter Armenian unity, especially at a moment like this when more than ever it was crucial to have general cohesiveness, unity, and love in the struggle against the domination of foreigners. Instead, the preaching of Gospel love and brotherhood by the missionaries had led, among Armenians, to nothing but hate and enmity.

"Missionaries have no regard for national identity," Sako went on.

"They just go and use whatever language a particular people speaks and understands the best to preach to them and instruct their children in. If they find Armenians speaking Kurdish somewhere, they preach to them in Kurdish. If they are Turkish speaking, then they preach to them in Turkish. What do they care what their mother tongue was? They'd never consider teaching Armenians their mother tongue in order to preach to them in it. So, from that point of view the work your organization is doing is very positive. It's the most effective way of making those people Armenian and keeping them so. A people's connection with its literature, its past, its historic life, and all its intellectual and spiritual expression through the ages – its entire existence – is based on its language. That's the tie that binds the individual to the whole nation. And as for the church, you can see from the examples I mentioned how weak it is in binding Armenians to their national identity, if they've lost that other more fundamental basis of national life, their language."

Sako appeared to me in a new light now and spoke in a way I had never heard before. He wasn't the same man I had first encountered in an Arab minaret, nor the merry joker who used to bore me in The Hunter's home. He spoke now like Aslan spoke, and I was struck at how similar in orientation and thinking these young men were.

"I agree completely," said the other young man who had been silent up to that point.

"But, even so, if our clerics had been legitimate, foreign preachers couldn't have been as harmful as they've been to us. If a wolf gets hold of one sheep from a flock, that shows that the shepherd and the dogs are no good. We have ignorant and uneducated priests, and our vartabeds think they're rendering the nation a great service by shutting themselves away in monasteries to engage in prayer and asceticism."

Just at this instance a certain gentleman passed close to our table, and all conversation suddenly halted. People at other tables reacted in the same way, and if he happened to sit down at any particular table the people who had been there would gradually move away.

"That man's a well-known spy," said Sako, indicating the man. "What nationality is he?" I asked.

"An Armenian, and what's more an 'effendi' with several different titles."

"So he betrays Armenians?"

"Who else?"

The "effendi" joined a group of young men the same age as himself and called for a round of drinks at his expense.

"I'll bet anything that good-for-nothing will any moment launch into patriotic utterances and start singing his own verses in which you'll hear 'Oh Armenia' over and over again," said Aslan.

But none of that happened, since it was quite late in the evening now, the customers were gradually drifting away, and Brother Teos was getting ready to extinguish the lamps. The noisy hall was soon empty. As he was about to extinguish the last two lamps, the two young men got up, said goodnight to me and Sako and disappeared into a dark corner of the coffeehouse. There they lay down right in the open on the bare wooden seats and rested their heads on their traveling bags. Brother Teos was too kind to throw them out into the street, or make the point that his coffeehouse was not meant to be an inn. It was with great sadness that I left them there. 'These poor young men,' I thought – 'so homeless, so abandoned, wandering from town to town to try helping a fallen people. You have to compete with foreign missionaries deployed in force, I thought. You have to struggle against people who live in mansions and pass out money as if it were dust to blind everyone. . . But there is something inside of you that is higher and stronger than all the glory and power enjoyed by those foreigners, and that is your deep love for the work you do.'

On returning to the room where I had left Aslan I found Sako with him. Sako had apparently slipped out of the coffee house through the rear door in order to meet Aslan. But who had let him know that Aslan was there. . . ?

Varak

It still remained for us to visit Varak Monastery. With that our explorations in Van would be complete.

It was a beautiful bright morning when, mounted on our horses, I and Aslan emerged from the tree-lined streets of Aykesdan[*] to set out for the monastery. Before us stood the breathtaking vista of Mt. Varak. It was just daybreak and little by little the sun rose up from "Galilee," the peak of Mt. Varak. I had never seen such an amazing sunrise. It seemed as if the sun had taken its nightly rest on "Galilee," in one of those caves that Hripsimé and her companions had taken refuge in centuries ago, and now rose up to shed its splendor on the land of the Armenians. The pure maiden had practiced her austerities in those very caves, then emerged like a bright light and was sent to Ararat to battle the heathen Armenian king and the darkness of paganism. It was out of this struggle that Christianity gained its first foothold in Armenia, and it was in these very caves that Hripsimé had hidden the life-giving holy remnant of the Cross that was embedded in the center of the little cross she wore around her neck. That relic had not been seen by anyone for all of four centuries and had remained hidden until it finally came into the open again through the unceasing prayers of Todik the Ascetic. Beneath the splendorous light of the sun it then flew down from the heights of the mountain, there to settle on its slope and become the adornment of Mt. Varak's earthly bosom, just as it had once been the adornment of Hripsimé's breast. In this very place churches were built that took the collective name Holy Cross, based on the holy relic, and it was these churches as a group that constituted Varak Monastery, our destination that morning.

The sun rose higher and spread its brilliance over all of Van in fiery bands of light that spanned the violet surface of the lake and illumined the far-off mountains still shrouded in their morning mist. I was entranced. The sunrise and mountains of this sacred land rekindled ancient memories in my heart. It seemed that the centuries melted away

---

*. This was the large suburb around the old city of Van.

as the ancient tradition came to life before my very eyes, exactly as Todik had seen it in his awesome vision.

The life-giving holy relic sailed down from the peak of Mt. Varak and radiated twelve pillars of light that touched the ground at twelve points, remaining in place long enough to be seen by the rulers and people. Two descended to the spots where St. Gregory and Garmravor Monasteries were built. Three touched down at Upper Varak, known as Galilee, and seven at Lower Varak. Each of the latter seven churches had its own name, but collectively they took the name of the mountain and were called Varak Monastery.

The day of the holy relic's first appearance was designated a feast day by the Armenian church and it has remained so up to our own time. From that day forward Varak became the holy Zion of Armenia's mountains, it's summit, its slopes, its lowlands covered with monasteries filled with monks. The holy relic was kept in Varak Monastery for long years, while pilgrims came from far and wide to worship it. Rich and poor alike lavished gifts of silver and gold upon it, and consecrated their lives and possessions to those who served it, all in order to preserve the prosperity and fabled glory of this sacred place. Here the monks were revered by the people and, in turn, offered their prayers for the world.

Gagik Ardzruni spent huge amounts of his own fortune to create a golden case and reliquarium to house the holy relic. Prince Ashod, his son, spent thirty thousand gold pieces to further adorn the reliquarium with pearls and other precious gems. When Senekerim, the last of the Ardzruni kings, was obliged to surrender his throne to the Byzantine Emperor and move to Sepastia, he took the holy relic with him. Then the holy relic was returned to Van together with the body of the unfortunate monarch. After that, it became an object pursued by various greedy tyrants. In 1651, it was carried off together with all the wealth of Varak by the Kurdish bandit leader Suleyman who took it back with him to Khoshap fortress which was the seat of his rule. All the centuries-long sacrifices for the holy relic that the devout masses had offered were brought to nought within a few short days. Suleyman held possession of the relic for four years, and the people of Van mourned its loss for that entire period of time. They sent many delegations with large ransoms to retrieve it until, at last, they succeeded and brought back this object so sacred to their life.

We were now ascending toward the summit of Mt. Varak. Its slope was richly green up to timberline, with bushes, groves of trees, meadows with thick grass. There were many amber fields of ripened barley and wheat on its flanks. The harvester is at work, his sickle gleaming in the sun, and his melancholy song ringing through the sacred environs of this gigantic and holy mountain.

Though still early morning the sun is already starting to scorch the earth. The shepherd stops on his way. He takes off his coat and drapes it over his walking stick to form an umbrella to protect himself from its withering rays, then sits and shelters in its shade. His sheep are spread out all around him grazing in the lush green grass. His goats are playfully darting from one end of the flock to the other, while the dogs look gravely on from afar, keenly watching over this innocent merriment, this reckless gayety that in a single instant can change to grief. . .

Mt. Varak is the water source for the valley of Van: countless streams originate there and supply water for all the villages scattered around its slopes, and then flow on to Van to irrigate the vast orchards and vineyards of its Aykesdan.

We were still a considerable distance from the monastery when we noticed a group of men in a field apparently engaged in some kind of agricultural experiment. The plow they were using was quite different from the very heavy type customarily used in this region.

Judging from the way he was dressed, the man guiding the plow wasn't a layman. He was showing some of the field workers from the monastery how to operate the new plow, and they looked on with interest. As we passed by we wished them well with the traditional local greeting. Discerning that we were on our way to the monastery, one of the young monks left the group and came over to lead us there.[*]

"Will we find Hairig here?" Aslan asked our guide as we drew near the monastery, referring to the abbot of the monastery. "Didn't you recognize him back there? That was Hairig, the man working the plow," the monk said, surprised at the question. "What kind of plow was that?"

"Hairig sent for it from Europe, and today was the first time we tested it. We hope to be getting other farming equipment, too."

"Does the monastery make a living from agriculture?"

*. This man was the famous Karekin Srvantsdiants, an important figure in the 19th century Armenian national renaissance.

"Yes, we farm our own land. But we also have a school of agriculture."

"Will Hairig be returning to the monastery shortly?"

"Yes, very soon. When he saw that you were on your way there, he sent me to escort you and make you comfortable until his return."

When we reached the monastery and entered the main gate, the majestic architecture on these venerable, sacred grounds came gradually into view and I could see, even at a glance, that this place was the entire antithesis of stark, ascetic monasteries. There was an entirely different atmosphere here, a breath of new life, an intimation of the union of the spiritual and the earthly.

The monastery had numerous gardens and was lined with trees both inside and outside its walls. Brooks of cold clear water flowed together to form the loud torrent that turned the great watermill.

"Hairig planted the trees himself. He repaired the watermill. It had stood broken and idle for years," said our guide.

As he led us into an immaculate and well appointed room, the young monk eagerly and cordially questioned us on a number of points: where we were from and where were we going, how much longer the good doctor would be in Van, his nationality, how many languages he spoke, etc. Aslan couldn't have been offended by his sincere curiosity.

"Has Hairig been the abbot here for long?" asked Aslan.

"No, but in the short time he's been here, he's done more than ten others could have done in twenty years' time, no matter how hard they tried."

Our young guide was one of Hairig's apostles. This was when I first noticed how his followers never spoke of him except with the deepest of feelings, nor uttered his name but with the greatest respect, something I saw repeated again and again afterwards.

"The monastery was in ruins before Hairig took over. There wasn't a school or any basic economy," our young guide went on. "Its product was stolen by internal and external thieves. It was choked with taxes."

The Turkish tax farmers even took the Holy Relic away.[*] But Hairig brought the monastery back to life. What you see is the fruit of his work. And what does he get in return for all that? Nothing but hatred, persecution, and treachery from his benighted enemies. . ."

---

[*]. Turkish tax farmers or tax farming was the practice whereby the central government auctioned the right to collect taxes in its name to certain individuals. This led to extortion and oppression.

There was a tremor in the young monk's voice as he uttered these last words. He went on to tell me about a terrible incident that had occurred just a few days earlier: As Hairig was on his way to Van he encountered a Kurdish outlaw on the road. When he looked the man straight in the face with his eagle eyes, the outlaw fell into confusion and started to tremble.

"Why are you so upset, my friend?" asked Hairig with his usual warm smile.

"I was about to kill you," said the outlaw as he knelt down and clutched Hairig's feet. "Why didn't you do it, then?" asked Hairig, raising the man up.

"Because God held my hand back," said the man.

The outlaw explained that he had been paid by Hairig's enemies to carry out the assassination but that, despite his promise to do so, his conscience had whispered that it was wrong to raise a sword against one of God's blessed ones.

"Well, you will be blessed, too. Go in peace now, and make sure you tell no one what you just told me," said Hairig

"Do you have mercy even on your enemies?" the outlaw asked in disbelief. "That is what God commands," said Hairig.

But despite Hairig's admonition the outlaw made no secret of who had been plotting his death and named names, so that the whole city found out.

"Who were they?" aked Aslan.

"Several churchmen in cahoots with some of the richest men in town and led by the prelate himself," responded the monk.

"What did he do to provoke such hatred that they were willing to have innocent blood on their hands?" asked Aslan with shock in his voice. "Could education and the light of culture be that odious to them?"

"Their feelings had nothing to do with education. How could they be hostile to something they had no inkling of. No, their reasons were purely economic. As I said a while ago, there was nothing like an economic base here for a long time. The monastery's wealth was squandered away by the monks themselves. Whatever they left was gobbled up by the prelate. When Hairig took over, he cleaned out the riffraff and brought in a higher caliber of monks. From that point on, all the product of the monastery went into sustaining the new institutions he founded here. After all of that, it's little wonder that the men who had been fleecing the monastery for so long would become Hairig's enemies."

"But doesn't he have anyone on his side?"

"He does, but no one with the power and influence his enemies have. The people on his side are those who've been persecuted and robbed and deprived of their rights. His friends are the poverty-stricken peasants, the tradesmen in town, the homeless, the displaced, and the helpless, plus some idealistic young people who want to do good but have no means to do so."

As to Hairig's standing in terms of ecclesiastical rank, he was just a vartabed. But despite the young monk's point about the economic motivations of his enemies, given all Hairig had accomplished and the fame he had won, as well as the great esteem in which he was held by the people, churchmen of higher rank could not help but be jealous of him. The new institutions he had founded, precisely because of their newness, were bound to seem alien and threatening to them. He had started a night school in the monastery, a kind of teachers' college. Here, young people from all over were brought together to be trained as teachers or well educated pastors, and then return to work in their native towns and villages. In Hairig's thinking, it wasn't enough just to teach reading, writing, and arithmetic, or just serve the people's religious needs. They needed just as much to know how to successfully manage their farms and care for their animals to attain higher productivity.

Beyond the school, Hairig hadn't overlooked the next stage of culture, the printing press. This press printed a number of schoolbooks, but also several books written in the vernacular in order to encourage the spread of literacy among the populace, and a monthly journal with most of the editorial work done by his monks.

Given the immensity of the work and the extreme hardships involved, only a man of Hairig's iron will could have succeeded in struggling against the odds to bring these projects to completion. How many trips he had made on foot to Bolis to knock on the doors of the wealthy amirahs, seeking their help for his projects! All of this he did on his own. He set the first example, and turned a rest home for profligate monks into such a first rate institution that it advanced the religious, ethical, and intellectual development of the people.

How eager was I to see this man, to hear his voice, to speak with him! And he didn't keep us waiting for very long. He left his plow in the field and returned promptly all covered in sweat and dust. He hurried to his room for a moment to wash up then came back to see us. He was in a good mood, because his first experiment with the new plow turned out to be very promising.

Hairig was still a young man, not a day over thirty-six. Being called "Hairig" at this young age would have seemed quite odd, except for the fact that he possessed all the fastidious concern and virtuous qualities of a loving father in relation to his monastery and the people. It didn't seem that fasting and constant prayer, these practices regarded as the core of life in our isolated monasteries, had harmed his physical vigor in the least, for he was sturdy and tall. He went without the traditional black hood of vartabeds. His dense auburn hair, which covered half of his forehead, was swept back carelessly onto his strong shoulders. His beard was as thick as a lion's main. The most striking feature of his pleasing though virile face were his large, eagle-like eyes and his eagle's beak of a nose, both reflecting the acute vision and sense of smell of that noble king of birds. It was for that reason he had earned his second name, "The Eagle of Vasbouragan."

His clothing was modest, and he was entirely ordinary and authentic in manner. Looking at this churchman and taking his past and his present into account, one immediately discerned his love for the common people. One saw a person who had lived humbly in a country cottage and was endowed with the simple, unselfish purity of a common peasant. One saw a priest filled with the inspiration of the highest ideals, who found the spiritual consolation of his work a search for the peace and progress of that very same common man, that peasant who had suffered for centuries. He was a man of the people, born for the people.

I had never met such a fine person before. He was the kind of monk who always mentioned the names of our national forefathers along with those of Jesus, Moses, and St. Paul, and that not only in ordinary conversation but in his sermons, too.

Biblical Palestine or "Supernal Jerusalem" didn't figure into what he talked about, for his promised land was Vasbouragan.[*] In him, love for his nation had become a consuming zeal, and religious devotion had reached the highest level of purity.

Seeing him brought to mind a certain fifth century monk freshly returned from his trip to Athens and, staff in hand like a wandering dervish, journeying to every corner of his homeland to shed the light and

---

[*]. This was the historic Armenian province in which the city of Van is located and considered by many as the cradle of Armenian civilization.

consciousness he had brought from the great cities of Greece, from Socrates and Aristotle. But his homeland wasn't ready for this new apostle of civilization, and the most ignorant class of monks were extremely hostile to him. But disregarding their benighted attacks, he carried his sacred mission forward with firm and noble resolve. Persecuted on all sides, he showed up each day in yet another place to plant the seeds of virtue he had brought with him in the intellectual desert created by his brethren. Hairig had so arranged his work that all of Vasbouragan was his own farm and he its diligent tiller.

He was a man truly beloved in his native land, Vasbouragan. Varak, Van, the lake and countryside all around were the beautiful objects of his contemplation. But he found himself in just the same situation as had Movses Khorenatsi[*] in his native Daron, for monks had also plotted against him. With this in mind, as well as the unfortunate episode a few days earlier, Aslan congratulated Hairig, and then added:

"Don't be disheartened, Hairig. Apostleship always involves martyrdom."

"Such incidents can't discourage me, doctor. I'm not afraid to die, but I don't want to, because people who have a lot of work to do need to live on."

A long conversation ensued which I don't wish to detail here. Then Aslan asked Hairig if he would show us the various projects the monastery was engaged in.

"We're just in the beginning stages, doctor, so we don't have much to show guests. Almost everything is still in its adolescence."

"Nevertheless what is already evident shows great promise for the future with its vigor and sound formation, at least physically," said Aslan.

"That's true, but even the healthiest children can turn weak and deformed in the hands of bad nursemaids and stepmothers."

We left the room. The monastery grounds were empty except for two doves flitting through the verdant beauty of the gardens. On seeing us they flew up to the bell tower and settled on a beam there. No other monastery had such serene sounding bells as these. At the Gdouts[†] monastery the bells rang all the time prodding the "ever-worshipful"

---

[*]. Movses Khorenatsi ("Moses of Khoren") has been called the "father of Armenian historiography"; the leading Armenian historian of the Middle Ages.

[†]. Gdouts monastery was a monastic order based on an island on Lake Van.

monks to continue their religious routine, whereas here one only heard them when announcing the break between classes.

The students came out in groups, and the silence that had prevailed beneath the towers of the monastery was broken by a lively clamor. Nothing cold be lovelier than the sound of these voices, issuing as they did from the hearts and souls of a new generation of children, a sound that would echo into the future. . .

Hairig led us to the library. It consisted of three rooms joined by doors. On entering the first room, he said:

"This is our entire collection of printed works, both in Armenian and foreign languages. All our brothers can come here at designated times and take advantage of the collection."

The room was well lit, with a long desk in the center covered with green woolen cloth. On it were copies of recently acquired newspapers and journals. The walls were lined with books, organized in large wooden bookcases behind glass. Everywhere I looked I saw order, good taste, cleanliness, and simplicity. This was not just a library, but a reading room.

We left this room to go into the next one.

"This is the collection of all our manuscripts," said Hairig.

This room was similar in arrangement to the previous one, the long desk in the center similarly covered in green cloth and surrounded by large wooden bookcases with glass doors. In them one could see the manuscripts produced by the constant toil of our forefathers. Pictures of St. Sahak and St. Mesrop hung in gilded frames in front of the room, these men who had given the Armenians letters and literature in their mother tongue. . .

Regrettably I couldn't help but think of the dark, dank sacristy of the Gdouts monastery where we had found the rarest specimens of ancient manuscripts scattered in one corner of the room covered in dust. How could one compare the two!

"Do you have a catalogue of the books, Hairig?" Aslan asked. "Yes, we do," said Hairig taking a book from one of the bookcases.

"We haven't printed it yet because we're always adding to the collection and want it to be as large as possible." Aslan sat down at the desk to look over the catalogue.

"Even so, you have a great many," he said. "You'd do me a great favor, Hairig, if you collected all the manuscripts from the surrounding monasteries and stored them here."

At that point Aslan told Hairig about our visit to the Gdouts monastery and the terrible disarray in which we had found its manuscripts.

"All the monasteries are like that," said Hairig. "If you only knew what I had to go through just to get these books together, all the troubles, all the unpleasantness! Our abbots would rather let their manuscripts go neglected and decay into nothing than let us have them and care for them properly. Now the common folk have a completely different way of relating to manuscripts. If they find one, they go and bury it in the ground as if they are burying their own children."

Aslan continued looking over the catalogue.

"Choristers do that, too," said Aslan. "I heard that a complete burial ceremony was held in a certain monastery to bury worm-eaten manuscripts."

"I know of another incident even worse than that," Hairig said sadly and began to recount the story:

In one isolated monastery on an island in one of Armenia's lakes the monastic community suddenly received word that the Catholicos would soon be visiting their monastery. In order to prevent his seeing the terrible condition their manuscripts were in, they gathered them all together, put them in jugs and dumped them into the lake. As the Catholicos was being brought toward the island in a boat, he noted vellum pages bobbing around in the water near his boat. One of them was born along on a wave and hit up against the side of the boat. The Catholicos reached down and picked the pitiful page of vellum out of the water. As it happened, this page was the very one on which Khorenatsi had put down his bitter lament on the perverseness of his fellow monks. Sitting right next to him in the boat was his host, the abbot of the very monastery he was going to visit who had come ashore to receive him. The Catholicos handed his host the page on which were written the lines beginning, "the fatuous vartabeds," etc.

"That story is as depressing as it is interesting," said Aslan. "But I've heard that one of your Catholicoi was tainted by a similar kind of sin as well: He had all his predecessors' papers burned in order to expunge any memory of them. But happily your catalogue shows not only the titles of books, but a whole list of royal declarations, decrees, and tax levies of numerous Persian and Turkish monarchs, all of which have great historical value."

There was a special bookcase in the library for the earliest copies of printed works in Armenian that came from Venice, Rome, Milan, New Jugha, Amsterdam and other places.

After looking over the manuscripts, we went into a third room which was much larger than the previous one.

"This is our museum, but it's very limited so far because we've just started it," said Hairig. Despite Hairig's modesty this room fascinated me far more than the others. What a rich collection it was! Every relic discovered in the area of Van and its surrounding ruins was to be found here. An assortment of ancient money was in cases under glass. There was also a collection of women's jewelry, such as earrings, necklaces, beads, etc. In another case were ancient, heavy bronze shields embellished with cuneiform inscriptions and legendary coats of arms, spearheads and arrowheads, pieces of barrels, and bronze helmets and body armor. But two objects in the collection fascinated me beyond all the rest, two statuettes: one was the gilded form of a young woman so beautiful I was ready to go down on my knees to worship it. Noticing the spell it cast over me, Hairig, with a smile on his face said to me, "We were once accused of committing that very same sin."

"What do you mean?" asked Aslan.

Hairig answered by telling us about some very disturbing incidents that had happened in connection with the museum. The museum's purpose was to bring together all the antiquities so plentiful in Van, but these were often destroyed by the common people before they reached the museum because they they had no idea of their value. For instance, a peasant once found the iron fragment of a pagan altar and took it to a blacksmith to have it broken up and made into a plow blade. Another peasant found the ivory feet of King Senekerim's[*] throne and sold it for a very low price to a gunmaker to make into pistol handles. The two statuettes we had seen in the museum were found just a few years before, and Hairig had barely been able to rescue them from the wrath of a mob that had surrounded him fully prepared to pulverize them, shouting, "Those are idols! !" It wasn't clear which goddess one of them was, but the other one, the one with the sparkling stars, was thought to be the queen

---

[*]. King Senekerim of the Ardzruni dynasty, the last king of Vasbouragan (in the 10th century). Lim monastery (leem) – Located on Lim island in Lake Van (present-day Turkish: "Adir" island).

of Van, the goddess Asdghig.* The statuettes were placed in the best lit part of the room near a picture of the Holy Mother of God. Within a few days an infuriated mob had descended on the monastery and came close to destroying the museum and everything in it. Pleading at great length with the enraged rabble, Hairig was barely able to mollify them, for they were riled up by their conviction that the museum was nothing but a site where idols were worshipped, with the Holy Mother of God alongside them as just another pagan goddess.

"The simple masses might have ideas like that," said Hairig, "But unfortunately it was some of my enemies among my fellow clerics who incited them to it. I don't think they did it malevolently or to harm our monastery, but because they were convinced that we couldn't have brought the statues here and placed them beside the picture of the Holy Mother for any other reason."

"And if they come across statues of the gods, what will they do?" asked Aslan, his eyes fixed on the picture of the Holy Mother, the focus of the discussion.

"They'll totally destroy them and reduce them to dust."

"But this Holy Mother is really stunning," said Aslan, continuing to gaze at the picture before him. "It has all the marks of a great fifteenth century Italian master. It amazes me how it ended up here."

"It's very likely that it was brought here in the period when the merchants of Van had close relations with Venice and Italy," said Hairig.

"But guess where I found it."

"Where?"

"In the ruins of a village church. All the Armenian villagers had been dispersed and Kurds were living there instead. But these people had kept their faith in the church and its sacred objects, perhaps because some of them were of Armenian origin."

This picture of the Holy Mother they were so passionately discussing didn't really capture my interest, perhaps because I had no understanding of art at all. The colors of the painting had long ago turned dark with the passage of time and with exposure to incense and candle smoke. One spot on the picture, the feet of baby Jesus in His Mother's arms, had been scorched, apparently by a carelessly set candle falling against it, and it was torn in another spot.

_____

*. Asdghig is the Armenian goddess Venus.

Hairig showed us another antiquity donated to the monastery, a piece of handiwork which, according to him, had been made by one of the Ardzrouni princesses, a beautiful table cloth on which the skillful maiden had created various scenes from the torture of St. Gregory.

"It often happens in our monasteries and churches that handiwork like this, or vestments and other such objects, fall out of use and become neglected. They're stored in closets as supposedly worn out and useless and there they languish and decay. Sometimes the most precious of artifacts can be found among them, ecclesiastical articles that had been brought here from distant lands such as India, China, and Isfahan by Armenian merchants.

Hairig next showed us his school which had its own special location on the monastery grounds. Until that day I had only seen two schools, Father Todik's, that frightful hell in which I had had the misfortune of being a pupil, and the other in Van which was different in form. But both of them, although located in two different countries, were the very archetypes of Armenian schooling, a system designed to dull the student's mind and lead to his psychological and intellectual death. These being the kind of schools I had seen, Hairig's school seemed totally like one of the Seven Wonders of the World to me. It was, indeed, the first of its kind in the country, its very newness making it a target for so much persecution. Of course, I was in no position to assess the substance of its teaching methods or curriculum. I was only judging by what I saw. For the first time, I saw pupils sitting in orderly rows on benches, so unlike Father Todik's school where pupils sat in a jumble on the floor on whatever piece of cloth, rug, or hide they had managed to bring with them from home. Here for the first time, I saw pupils divided into classes, each with its own teacher. In father Todik's school, quite the opposite was the case, with no consideration given to age or level of learning. All the pupils were mixed together in the same room like sheep in a fold. Father Todik would go from one pupil to the next, helping one with handwriting, another with reading, while another one was cleaning the teacher's shoes for him. In a word, there were as many grades in the class as there were pupils. But in Hairig's school I saw chalk and blackboard being used for the first time, and pupils who learned their lessons without corporal punishment, in a classroom without a trace of the *falaka* or whips or other disciplinary instruments of Father Todik's school.

After showing us all the classrooms, Hairig led us to the main hall where there were many natural specimens on display: minerals, dried insects, colorful butterflies, and numerous dried plants and flowers that were so well preserved that they had lost none of their form or beauty. There was also a number of stuffed birds that looked totally alive to me.

"Our students collected all of these things, doctor," Hairig said with such enthusiasm you would have thought he was delighting in the firstborn of his students. "Sometimes they go on little excursions into the mountains with their teachers so that they can learn about nature by being in it."

"That has to be a great step forward, Hairig, teaching your pupils natural sciences instead of burdening their minds with dark theological questions," said Aslan.

"I'm convinced, doctor, that it's as important to make fine technicians and agriculturists of our students as it is to make good Christians of them. Our people are destitute and hungry. They need to be taught how to feed themselves. That's why I added agriculture to the curriculum. And if that goes well, I'll eventually start a technical institute. My monastery's protective saints are kind and forgiving; the noise of saws and hammers doesn't bother them." Having said that, he added, "I don't mean to completely dismiss the cultivation of the soul, quite the contrary; that requires even more attention."

With this he launched into a lengthy explanation: Besides the tremendous losses incurred as a result of the population emigrating to other countries, another grave blow to the moral fabric of Vasbouragan was the host of aberrations that the returning emigrants brought back with them to their still pristine homeland. The sacred propriety and order of old was lost and people fell into impure ways. What they needed now was moral cleansing. Obviously that was the primary task of religious educators. True religion and a well designed spiritual education in church, school, and home can be effective in giving children the moral guidance they need.

Having shown us all the main enterprises of the monastery, Hairig led us to his room where we found a simple meal waiting for us. As we sat down to eat, he continued talking about education in the monastery.

"There are many people who are opposed to education being offered in monasteries, thinking that a monastery, with its gloomy domes and its pictures of ancient martyrs and ascetics, is no place to prepare a new generation for the world. That would be true if the Armenian monastery were like others. But, whether in the past or the present, its great distinction is that it has never severed the link that binds it to the people and gone off to serve its own needs aside from theirs. There have been a few exceptions, monasteries founded on exclusively monastic principles, but these are alien to the values of the Armenian people and never last," he said.

"And why shouldn't we make the most of our monasteries? Our forebears poured their money into them, they turned their most precious possessions over to them, and most of that wealth is still here. It used to be spent on charity, but now it's spent to educate the people so that what came from them can be given back."

"But is education enough, Hairig?" asked Aslan.

"No, it's not enough. Educating children but failing to provide them with a livelihood will only result in their becoming educated sufferers. In that case, one simply becomes more aware of one's poverty, because the greater one's intellectual development, the greater one's needs. A common person is satisfied with a crust of bread, but once you educate him he realizes that meat is more nourishing. And what a dark day it will be for him when he can't find any!"

I was struck by this churchman's arguments, ideas that ran totally counter to that of most clerics. He didn't harp on the vanity of worldly desires or condemn life's pleasures on the grounds that one had to negate the body in order to gain the true happiness of heaven.

"Yes," said Aslan, "Education has to be a means of providing for life's real needs. But let me ask you this, Hairig, what do you think the people need more than anything else right now? To put it another way, what would you say is their greatest impediment, the main problem that has to be solved?"

With this question, there was a total transformation in Hairig's mood. His expression clouded over and he turned very somber.

"What our people are suffering from is so vast and complicated it's impossible to express in a few simple words, doctor. As a physician you know that when you're confronted by many diseases at the same time, you have to focus on the one that is causing the most death."

"That's true, but what disease would that be?"

"As I see it, it is exodus," said Hairig, and with this he began to talk at length on this subject, stating that some way had to be found for the Armenians to make a living in their own land.

"It's obvious why Europeans emigrate. They have so many people and so little land, there isn't enough land for everyone. But here we have a vast land, yet it doesn't do the people any good."

"But why?" asked Aslan.

"There are many, many reasons, doctor: agriculture is stuck in its primitive stage; the agrarian laborers, the most productive part of our population, are robbed of their living by a host of injustices; the roads are dangerous and unfit for export. And there's not a single organization or institution in the country devoted to promoting economic development. I ask you, doctor, which of these evils is the worst?"

"Under those circumstances, what hope can there be for progress?" asked Aslan.

The discussion now took up the question whether it was possible for the Armenians simply to devote themselves to peaceful labor and get on with their lives when the government – far from being helpful – itself threw barriers in the way of progress and at the same time gave free rein to every whim of the Muslim population so that Armenian life and property were placed under constant threat.

"Given our unfortunate circumstances, it's a fact that the people can't simply give themselves over to undisturbed labor," said Hairig. "That's the main reason so many of them forsake their homeland and go to seek a living elsewhere. But can all the blame be placed on those who rob others of the fruits of their labor? Those who allow themselves to be robbed in that way are just as responsible. I'm convinced that a Kurdish bandit would never get near an Armenian's flock if he knew he'd find the owner standing guard with a rifle in his hands."

"I agree," said Aslan. "But men of the cloth have a great deal of influence. Why don't they preach a modicum of self-defense to the population. After all, in the East religion and religious leaders are always in the thick of mass movements and will always play an essential part in them."

At this Hairig grew somber once more.

"I have no such expectations of my fellow clerics. They'll never preach self-defense. As things stand, I'd simply be thankful if they'd just stop preaching submission. But on the contrary, they place all their faith in the government and preach that it's up to the government to maintain order and provide for the people's welfare. But when the government is weak and has no control, how can it maintain order? They don't think about that. They think that everything will somehow work out on its own. . ."

Then Hairig began speaking with great regret about the treachery that had caused so much grief to the Armenians of Van for the last several decades, buffeting them with a host of evils. The people were divided into two parties: The leader of one was the local prelate in league with a number of the leading rich men of the city and a few traitorous effendis who had government positions; the leadership of the other party was a group of young people together with Hairig. And so – on one side, wealth and political power, on the other side, the harried, exploited masses. One side demanded blind obedience, while the other protested endless injustices.

Having heard all of this, it was obvious why the prelate and his allies would conspire against Hairig's life. Yet Hairig recounted it all in the most normal manner, without betraying the least sign of animosity. His equanimity stemmed not from indifference but from the greatness and purity of a soul who offered forgiveness to his enemies. Still, one couldn't help but detect a certain pain in his voice, a bitter pain buried deep in his heart. Why did it have to be like that, so much discord and duplicity and all the internal strife that dissipated the strength of good people? How much time had been wasted on those frustrations when, instead, they could have been achieving something truly worthwhile?

"This is what happens when the clergy either don't understand, or don't care to understand, that their true calling is to represent the church and serve all the faithful," Hairig went on. "This is what happens when they fail to understand that everything they do should promote harmony. That's where they go wrong. They become masters instead of servants and begin ordering others around and using them for their own personal ends. Then they ally themselves with the political establishment, which legitimizes their authority and backs them up, and the more chaotic it is the better for them. Therefore, how can we really be shocked that the prelate of Van has joined forces with the pasha to fleece the miserable populace. . ."

"I had a visit with the pasha. He seemed a very cunning man," said Aslan. "A very devious man, like all Turkish officials," said Hairig.

In the evening when it became cooler, Hairig led us on a long walk around the monastery, taking great pleasure in pointing out everything he had accomplished and hoped to accomplish in the future.

This passionate man appeared to me like a competent farmer familiar with everything that grew on his farm, who knew their nature, had studied their lives, and loved them the way a woman loves the flowers she has planted and raised with her own hands. He was pointing out various fields, saying:

"Over there we're beginning to cultivate *madder*,[*] the first time it's been tried in our region. It looks very promising. And look over there at those newly planted mulberry trees. With them we're going to try our hand at sericulture to produce our own silk. And did you know, doctor, that up until just a few years ago potatoes were entirely unheard of here? We were the first to cultivate them, and we've put a lot of work into spreading their cultivation to all the surrounding villages, as well. We've done such a good job, our priests still haven't had enough time to figure out whether the faithful are allowed to eat them on fasts or not!" Hairing quipped, causing Aslan to laugh.

"I've received a lot of criticism for starting an agricultural school here, doctor. Some people believe it's totally at odds with the purpose of a monastery and so on. But I ask you, who should know more about agriculture than monks? A monastery isn't just a place for prayer; it has an entire economy to maintain and expertise in agriculture is essential. If you look at the inscriptions on our walls you'll see that from ancient times right up to the present countless villages, farms, vineyards, and forests have been donated to our monasteries by everyone from kings and queens to the common faithful. That's why here, as throughout the rest of Armenia, those are the most valuable of all properties. How can the monasteries properly manage them without a knowledge of agricultural economy, and how else can they avoid being hoodwinked even by relatively honest tax collectors? And not only that, their lack of knowledge can result in the ruin of their properties, something that has already happened with several monasteries."

After listening intently to every word Hairig had said, Aslan had a question for him:

---

[*]. *Madder* is a plant cultivated to produce a bright red dye.

"But don't you think, Hairig, that with so much wealth at their command there's a risk that the monks will turn themselves into an educated and cultured élite?"

"What danger can come of being educated?" asked Hairig with obvious amazement.

"I mean the danger of clericalism," said Aslan. "Up to now, because of their low level of education, your monks have been fairly weak and harmless. But with education will come power, and with that power they'll try to lord it over the people and exploit them."

"That isn't likely with us, for 'clericalism' runs counter to the spirit of our church," responded Hairig. "Our church is genuinely popular in character, and if monks because of their education are in a position to take advantage of the people, then isn't it the case that the people will have been at least as well educated as they, and that a certain balance will be struck between them so that the one side can't overpower the other? Monks can only become dangerous when their level of culture far outstrips that of the people."

Aslan didn't want to prolong the discussion, because this was a highly controversial topic. The sun was already beginning to set. Hairig was in no hurry to terminate our excursion and seemed intent on keeping us in the monastery overnight. But Aslan graciously declined, saying he had a great deal of business to attend to in the city. On returning to the monastery, Aslan told me to immediately prepare the horses. I headed for the stables and left him talking to Hairig.

Betrayal

It was well past sunset by the time Aslan and I finally bid farewell to Hairig, and we made an easy descent from the monastery thanks to the level road that Hairig had built. Our guide down the mountain was a priest named Father Yeghishé. He and Aslan rode ahead of me, talking together as they went, and I followed well behind at a leisurely pace.

We arrived at Aykesdan in the middle of the night and Father Yeghishé invited us to his house for a meal. Aslan was usually averse to such invitations, but in this case he made an exception.

We enjoyed a very nice meal with Father Yeghishé, regaled by him with fascinating stories about Hairig, about the ignorance of the local clergy, and about his wide-ranging travels abroad.

"Do you think the lady will really be able visit?" Aslan asked our host when we were finished eating. "Don't worry, she'll be here soon enough," the priest replied.

"But it must be extremely difficult for her."

"She's very shrewd, she'll figure out a way."

The woman whose visit Aslan was so impatiently awaiting was Father Yeghishé's own sister, Telli-Khatoun. Two irretrievable losses had struck their family while Father Yeghishé was away from home on his travels: their mother died, and Telli-Khatoun, his only sister, was left alone and vulnerable. She was soon abducted from her home and forced to marry a local Turkish official. Despite the delicate situation in which she found herself, she never gave up doing whatever she could to protect her people and moderated her husband's extreme measures when she could. If a direct approach was out of the question then she resorted to clandestine methods to accomplish her ends.

When she finally arrived I could immediately see that she and Aslan were no strangers to each other. In a bold and extravagant gesture quite out of character for a woman of the harem, she came right over to Aslan with a bright smile on her face, sat down beside him and took his hand in hers.

"Oh, I so wanted to see you! Where have you been? Spending all your time wandering through monasteries, I suppose."

"What can I say? It's important to know what's going on inside those dark walls. After all, our people are still in bondage to them," said Aslan very cordially.

"But don't you know they're laying traps for you?"

"I know and that's exactly why I wanted to see you."

"You've been betrayed."

"I've been expecting that for a long time."

Telli-Khatoun then handed Aslan a letter. As he read it, his face registered a whole succession of extraordinary expressions. "How did this letter end up in your hands?" he asked when he had finally regained his composure.

Telli-Khatoun told him that the pasha's secretary had delivered it to her husband a few days earlier and entrusted it to him with the demand that everything possible be done to apprehend the person described. She overheard the conversation between the pasha's secretary and her husband and very soon realized who it was about. Taking advantage of her husband's absence, she slipped the letter from his papers and brought it with her.

It was written in Turkish and the gist of it was roughly the following:

A particular individual dressed as a monk had been spotted at the Festival of the Holy Mother of God, passing himself off as a reclusive mountain ascetic and circulating among the pilgrims. After that, the counterfeit monk changed into the garb of a Vanetsi merchant and spent a whole day in the tent of a Yezidi chieftain who was a well-known enemy of the government. After that the suspect disappeared, but the author of the letter considered it most likely that he went to Van.

The letter went on, "This crafty individual is a leading member of a large group of traitors who are stirring up trouble wherever they go. These scofflaws are quite audacious and their fanatical commitment to their cause makes them extremely dangerous. If this man is found in Van, he can definitely be expected to have assumed an entirely new disguise.

"I am obliged for the greater part of this information to the abbot of the Mother of God Monastery, Garabed Vartabed, who is one of our most faithful servants and personally known to your majesty, the same man whom you honored with a medal one year ago.

Through a happy coincidence, he was able to solve the mystery of the suspect's identity, but only after the suspect had left our area. I immediately sent my men after him, but they regrettably lost track of him."

The letter was addressed to the pasha of Van and signed by none other than the Kurdish chieftain, Sharif-Bek, whom we last saw at the monastery of the Holy Mother of God where he had come to take his cut of the gifts brought by the pilgrims. Below Sharif-Bek's signature also appeared the seals of Garabed Vartabed, Der-Todik, as well as my own Uncle Bedros, these accompanied by the following words: "We vouch with certainty for all the details the beg has reported and fully attest to them."

"You'd better take that letter and put it back where you found it before your husband finds it missing," said Aslan to Telli-Khatoun. "But tell me, do you remember the whole conversation between the secretary and your husband?"

"Yes."

"Who do they suspect?"

"You. My husband told the secretary, 'There's something fishy about that European doctor.' The secretary told him you had been invited to the prelate's as a guest. He said the pasha would also be there and that they were planning to question you. Is it true you received an invitation to the prelate's?"

"Yes."

"Well, I advise you not to go; it would be extremely risky for you."

"I have to go, precisely because they're planning to question me."

"But my husband will be there, too. He's a very dangerous man."

"Well, as they say, a fox in the chicken coop becomes a lion. Of course he's dangerous, but only to the pitiful Armenians here."

"You'd still better be careful."

"Don't worry, everything will be fine."

Trial

It was quite dark by the time Aslan and I mounted our horses and set off for the prelacy. "Don't you think the prelate will be suspicious of you?" I asked as we rode along.

"Of course he will. It's inconceivable the pasha wouldn't pass the information on to him."

"Then you didn't need that woman's warning?"

"Not at all."

"But if the prelate finds out you're the man they're looking for he'll have you arrested on the spot."

"That's true, but first he'll have to prove it's me!"

Seeing how sure of himself Aslan was I didn't say another word about the matter and he imparted his final instructions for our visit:

"When we are there just follow the usual pattern and take a position at the door. Then pay close attention to every word that's uttered."

When we arrived at the prelacy a group of servants stood waiting for us at the gate and took our horses in to take care of them. We were then escorted into the prelacy with the highest courtesy. Fully expecting to join the prelate at a modest meal befitting a man of the cloth, we were on the contrary led into a splendorously decorated hall. The lighting was so bright it dazzled our eyes. I had never seen such opulence. The prelate was seated in the most imposing part of the hall on a blanket of the finest velvet spread over a beautiful Persian rug. He wore a purple cloak for the occasion and a diamond studded badge bearing the Ottoman emblem glittered on his chest. He was flanked on his right by the pasha and on his left by an important Kurdish bek.

The prelate received me without moving from his spot and simply held out his hand to be kissed. But when Aslan approached he rose partway up and shook his hand very cordially and invited him to sit down next to the pasha. There were no chairs and everyone sat on rugs. I took my position to the left of the door and remained there, while the pasha's bodyguard stationed himself on the other side. We were both armed and kept our hands on our swords. It's a great honor for bodyguards to be stationed in the same room as their masters on important visits. The bodyguards or servants of commoners are customarily stationed in anterooms, as was the case with the Kurdish bek's bodyguard this evening.

After the customary greetings, which consisted of repeatedly lowering the hand to the waist and raising it to the forehead as a sign of respect, the pasha addressed himself to Aslan with a crude smile on his boorish face:

"Thanks to you, doctor, I'm completely well now. I had to come and thank you in person for your remarkable skill as a physician."

"I'm embarrassed, your majesty. Could my modest efforts have been so successful?"

"Very, very successful, doctor!" said the pasha, nodding his head emphatically. "Let me assure you, if I didn't know that Mohammed was the perfection of the prophets and followed by no others, I would have taken you for one of God's prophets sent into the world to perform miracles," he insisted with double-edged flattery.

"But the age of miracles is over, your majesty. We're living in an age of science and technical proficiency now, one that promises wonders even greater than the supernatural cures of old."

"I'm a believer, doctor, and for me the age of miracles is still with us. I suffered away in Stamboul for five years – for five whole years! – while all the Sultan's best physician's worked on me but without doing me a bit of good. Then with just a few of your medicines I was completely cured!" Aslan explained to me later that the pasha hadn't been sick at all and that the medicines he had given him were only placebos. It was more than likely that the cunning pasha had feigned illness just to detain Aslan in Van long enough to verify his suspicions about him. Whatever the case, extravagant flattery of this sort is not only common in the East but has become the very standard of politeness.

Aslan picked up the thread and, turning to the prelate, addressed him in the same manner:

"I can't thank you enough for your letter of recommendation, Reverend Father. It's made it possible for me to do everything I wanted to do."

"That was simply our obligation, doctor. We did whatever we could to help a visitor satisfy all his interests and get better acquainted with our country and people. My only regret is that I didn't have the chance to warn you how dangerous it could be to visit Gdouts Monastery. Though our lake isn't that large, it's very wild at times. I'm glad, very glad, that you courageously survived your ordeal. I can see that you're not only an outstanding physician but an accomplished mariner and swimmer, as well. I must say I was amazed at what I heard about your courage during the storm." said the prelate, making it clear that he was already well-informed about our adventure.

"Well, Reverend Father, in my country we are taught from earliest childhood how to confront a variety of dangers; it's part and parcel of our education. If you grow up living near the ocean you have to start learning how to deal with it as early as possible."

This entire conversation with all its ambivalent phrases was merely a form of verbal sparring, and, since Aslan only followed suit the prelate was forced to take a different tack:

"I heard you visited Varak Monastery, doctor. What did you think of it and all the new projects they have going on there? Did you have the chance to see Hairig?"

"Yes I did, I had a long visit with him. His monastery proves that monks are capable of serving as first-rate teachers if they're given the chance to do so."

"That's exactly my goal, doctor. I'm still not done with my plans for Varak. I'm working and will continue to work to bring all the monasteries in my jurisdiction in line with its example, if the resources are available. Our monasteries are in a very bad state because of the difficult times we're going through now, but I'm doing everything in my power to improve their condition."

These comments about Hairig and his monastery were completely hypocritical, coming as they did from the mouth of his biggest enemy. This prelate who had resorted to any and all means to destroy everything that Hairig had undertaken at Varak now shamelessly took credit for his achievements and initiatives. But the prelate made short shrift of this topic and abruptly dropped it for another:

"I've been so fascinated by you and your many adventures that I completely forgot to introduce you to my other guests. Now, that gentleman there is Sharif-Bek, the leader of one of the biggest and bravest Kurdish tribes," he said, pointing out the Kurdish chieftain.

"I'm very pleased to meet you," said Aslan, extending his hand to the beg.

"He's a very honorable man and one of my best friends," continued the prelate. "Thanks to him our border with Persia is completely calm and secure. He's a compassionate friend and protector of the Armenian populace."

I instantly recognized Sharif-Bek, and it was clear that Aslan recognized him even sooner. The last time we had laid eyes on this individual was at the Festival of the Holy Mother of God where he had come to oversee and divide up with Father Garabed the offerings brought to the monastery by the pilgrims. Not only that, but he was the very author of the letter of indictment against Aslan that we had seen the night before. It appeared that the pasha had summoned him that evening in order to confer with him.

"And this is Latif-Bek, the local chief of police, a very fine man thanks to whom our town enjoys complete tranquility," said the prelate, continuing with his introductions.

Aslan also extended his hand to this "very fine" man, the husband of Father Yeghishé's sister, Beli, the very man who had been given the assignment of apprehending the suspect in question. He was looking intently at Aslan the whole time from beneath his thick, bushy eyebrows. Sharif-Bek and Latif-Bek were armed. Taking a look at the latter, I thought of what a victim a good and decent woman like madame Beli must have been in the hands of such beast.

There weren't many other guests besides Sharif-Bek and Latif-Bek, just three others who were Armenians. Pointing out the first, the prelate said:

"This is one of the leading men in the Armenian community, Sharman Bek. All the management of government building projects is in his hands, a reflection of his great reliability. He received a decoration from the Sultan a short time ago."

And truly, a decoration glittered on Sharman-Bek's breast. As soon as I heard his name I was reminded of a fascinating story that Master Panos had told us about the construction of a military installation in Van. It was this very man, Sharman-Bek, who had indemnified the entire cost of construction to the Armenian populace and at the same time received payment for it from the government treasury which he then divided up with the pasha and a number of other officials. Reader, I must retell this story so that it is firmly etched in you memory:

Around Van and the region near the Persian frontier, Turkish border guards were normally quartered in Armenian homes because they had no barracks of their own. Every Armenian home was required to put up several such guests. Given these circumstances, the self-invited guest became lord and master of the house. The women and girls of the family became his maids and served him, and the boys took care of his horse for him. The lazy and insatiable Turkish soldier acquires an exceedingly fine taste in such circumstances and becomes extremely demanding when he has access to free food in an Armenian's home. If his demands are not instantly met he wreaks havoc on the family with his whip, and the very honor of the family is sacrificed to his raging impulses. Imagine for yourself a simple, traditional household where everyone lives in the same space, then throw a totally depraved Turkish soldier into the mix. The Armenian has learned to bear with every other kind of oppression, but when the honor of his family is at stake his patience runs out.

It was this that provoked the Armenian community to protest to the highest echelons of the government to get the soldiers out of their homes. On hearing their protests, the government response was to order barracks to be built for the troops at the expense of the various localities. With this a vast project opened up for Sharman-Bek, the administrator of government construction. He went to the gullible peasants and told them, "If you want the troops out of your homes, then you'll have to pay for building the barracks yourselves. That is what the government has ordered." The poor peasants would have undergone any hardship whatever just to be rid of their guests.

Those who had the money paid in money. Those who didn't donated their labor, using their own animals to haul rocks and timber and mortar. This was how the barracks got built. Sharman-Bek was rewarded for this great service with the large decoration he sported on his breast, though the project was paid for by the poor populace, on the one hand, and by the government, on the other.

"He's a very devout and patriotic man, doctor," added the prelate. "If you only knew how many good things he's done for the people. Not long ago he paid for the expense of rebuilding the dilapidated sanctuary of a monastery."

The last statement was true, but robbing the populace to rebuild sanctuaries can hardly be deemed a form of piety. Despite that, Sharman-Bek was visibly moved by the prelate's flattery. His hand went up to his breast as if to check that his decoration was still in its place, the hint of a self-satisfied smile playing over his swarthy face.

The prelate continued with his introductions:

"And this is Pilgrim Toros. He's made the pilgrimage to Jerusalem several times. He's one of our richest and most distinguished merchants and an elder of our church. He's rendered many great services to the church. Long life to him! He's a very pious man and completely dedicated to his community."

Aslan paid no attention to the man, and, as for me, I turned my face away to hide my smile. Guess who that "rich, very pious, patriotic merchant" was: the very same trickster who had come to see us in Aykesdan at Varbed Panos's house and presented fake money as genuine antiquities to sell to Aslan. He was dressed in rags on that occasion in order to arouse our pity for his deplorable condition. Yet now, though it was summer, he wore an expensive fox fur jacket and a broad Persian sash.

To avoid any embarrassment Aslan pretended that he didn't recognize him. It wasn't, in fact, so easy to recognize him, since he was now wearing a fez wrapped in the kind of kerchief called *hasmeh*. His wrinkled face had been carefully shaved and his nose, shaped like a camel's saddle, seemed to me even longer now and entirely overhung his upper lip. The only bit of truth in all the praise the prelate had heaped on him was that he was, indeed, a very rich man, given that he was the pasha's own banker. He lent the pasha whatever he wanted at the highest rate of interest and was paid back through taxes taken from the villagers. As to how he went about collecting these taxes, that was entirely dependent on his conscience – if, indeed, he had one.

The third individual the prelate introduced was a gnarled, hunchbacked old man who had twice made the pilgrimage to Jerusalem. He was accordingly named Mahdessi Haro. If one had never set eyes on Jesuits, this man's demeanor and speech were enough to give a good idea of what they were like. He was the leading goldsmith and jeweler of the town and on very close terms with the pasha whose harem he provided with jewelry. For some reason the prelate didn't use the words "pious and patriotic" about him, but called him "very distinguished." That didn't really surprise me since Armenian jewelers and goldsmiths had assumed considerable status in the courts of sultans and shahs and had frequent dealings with the influential overseers of the harems.

"These three gentlemen also sit on the municipal court," the prelate said in conclusion.

With these introductions over, the pasha began to engage Aslan's attention in various ways. He kept turning to him and addressing various witticisms and facetious comments to him, laughing while he did so even though there was nothing humorous in what he said.

"You must have found our local antiquities very interesting, doctor," he said.

"The antiquities? Oh yes, they were very interesting. But more recent things proved a real disappointment," said Aslan. The pasha either didn't understand or decided to ignore Aslan's point. The prelate answered for him:

"If you had seen our city ten years earlier, doctor, you would have seen it totally in ruins. Now things have been set right and are in good order. The people who live here enjoy complete safety and little by little the ruins are being repaired. We owe all of that to our august pasha here, whose governance has brought us progress and life."

"That's all so true. May God grant long life to the august pasha effendi," assented the Armenian notables in unison.

"Well, I'm very happy to hear that," replied Aslan. "I'm sure the august pasha effendi will find an appropriate place in my memoirs of this journey."

However one was to understand this "appropriate place," the pasha, to be sure, took it in its best sense. Pressing Aslan's hand and with a tenderness in his voice which was at odds with the severity of his expression, he said:

"Thank you for your kind words, doctor. Can I assume your memoirs will soon be published?"

"Without a doubt, and they will likely be translated into several languages."

Mahdesi Haro, the Armenian notable sitting closest to Aslan, bent forward to Aslan's ear as if to confide something in him, though everyone could hear what he said:

"He's a man worthy of the highest respect."

His narrow, wily eyes were totally lacking eyelashes and were framed only by thick, red eyelids.

"I'm an eighty year old man, doctor, and I've seen many things," he said turning toward the pasha. "The situation used to be very bad here, but now the wolf and the lamb get along, people leave their doors unlocked day and night. There's no longer any reason for them to lock their doors because robbers are no more. You can wear gold on your head in public and go wherever you want without fear. You're safe anywhere.

Whether in the cottages of the poor or in rich men's homes, all you hear is prayer and happiness. There's no discontent anywhere."

It was always the same flattery, the same endless, unmitigated hypocrisy. And now I understood the truth of what Aslan had said to me and Maro at the festival of the Holy Mother about the role the representatives of the people play in keeping them poor. Then, I had only heard about what the monks, the government officials, the financiers and their like did, but now I saw their living specimens. If Aslan had only been a consul, someone officially sent to investigate the conditions of the country, he certainly would never have seen the inside of a peasant cottage, nor met the starving inhabitants of the city. Anywhere he would go, he would meet with the same flattery. That being so, what impression of the country would he be left with? A good one, no doubt. Men in that role cause great evil at the highest levels of government. When the news of peoples' protests reaches the Sublime Port, when they voice their grievances against the many abuses of a pasha, a moutour, or a kaimakam, you'll see these sycophants gather their forces and send a flattering letter to Bolis. Everything is then nullified. The voices of the exploited are drowned out, because greater credibility is given to these representatives of the people, these "notables." The government's interests are bound up with the interests of such scoundrels, and they benefit from its protection.

It seemed that Aslan couldn't contain himself:

"Nevertheless, there are still disturbances. While I was traveling near the Persian frontier terrible barbarities were taking place. Some Chaldi Kurds had crossed the border and burned over ten Armenian villages; they stole their animals and killed the shepherds. These raids caused such terror there that caravans completely stopped traveling on the roads, the harvest was abandoned in the fields, and the farmers were afraid to come outdoors."

That story was true and had occurred just as he had described it. But I wondered why he had mentioned it at the risk of being found out; for seated right there was the leader of the tribe that had carried out those very raids, Sharif-Bek. Aslan acted as if he didn't know, and, as if to offend the man even more tellingly, added:

"I've set down all the information, and I'll definitely have to report it to the appropriate authorities."

This latter statement seemed highly unwise to me. Why did he say it at the risk of provoking the Kurdish beg into taking some action against him? Would the Kurdish chieftain simply allow him to forward the information? More likely, he would send one of his men to follow the messenger or Aslan himself and have him killed on the way. Aslan wanted to take his revenge against the beg, for not only had the Kurdish leader written a report to the pasha about Aslan, but had personally come to Van to help the pasha find him.

After Aslan's unexpected remarks the three Armenian 'notables' gave each other anxious looks, searching for some way to defend the Kurdish leader. The prelate, too, was seized with anxiety and the pasha didn't know how to defend his powerful ally.

But, showing as much competence in verbal exchange as boldness in his marauding exploits, he responded quite coolly: "What road did you take to get here, doctor? You're very lucky you escaped that situation without incident."

This is the start of the trial, I thought. The beg's question was framed with great cunning, and I waited in dread to see how Aslan would extricate himself.

"I was never in any danger at all," responded Aslan quite casually. "While I was still in the Erzeroum area, the French ambassador warned me about the unrest among the Kurds and obtained a letter of safe passage for me from the provincial governor. This letter authorized me to have as many mounted guards as I needed to escort me wherever I needed to go, so I was well protected."

"He did right, doctor; such precautions are always wise," said the beg, and, though he tried to cover it up, his tone betrayed the disappointment of a hunter whose bullet has missed its mark. "You must have traveled by way of Timar, then."

"No, I took the caravan route straight from Erzeroum to Bayazid, then went to Maku, where the disturbances I mentioned had occurred, and from there I went on to Tabriz. I then followed the eastern shore of Lake Urmia to the town of Urmia. From Urmia I proceeded to Bash-Galah, then took the Khoshap Valley road to Van."

The beg's frustration was compounded at this point, because the route described by Aslan totally bypassed the area where the suspect had been sighted. Nevertheless, he made another attempt:

"If you had left the Khoshap Valley and taken the Jol-Jiman road, you would certainly have come upon one of the important festivals at a famous Armenian monastery. That would have been something of great interest to you in your travels." The beg was referring to the Monastery of the Holy Mother of God where the suspect had been spotted.

"While I was passing through the area I heard that the festival was over and the pilgrims were already on their way back home," answered Aslan.

Given Aslan's response, the beg found his veiled line of interrogation suddenly blocked. Latif-Bek, the police chief, had remained silent up to this point but now turned to the pasha.

"Why don't we simply follow the good example the governor of Erzeroum set and provide the doctor with a similar letter of safe passage? After all, he's our guest here." Then, addressing Aslan, "If I'm not mistaken, you're going to leave Van in a couple of days, so we'll have to write the letter as soon as possible. All we need is for you to send us the governor's letter and we'll simply follow its form."

Aslan had fallen into a trap, I thought, for Latif-Bek had couched his demand to see the official letter in the politest terms. He wasn't content simply to take Aslan's word about an open letter from the governor of Erzeroum for free passage to this or that location, etc. Catching the point of Latif-Bek's words, the pasha cunningly backed-up his proposal:

"Yes, yes, the doctor's our honored guest! Though there's nothing to be afraid of in our province, we're obligated to do our utmost to facilitate his travels and ensure his safety here."

"I'm grateful for your concern, esteemed lord," said Aslan, with a respectful nod to the pasha. "You've been so kind and thoughtful. You've generously offered me your hospitality even without seeing the letter first."

A rather dumbfounded look suddenly crossed the pasha's fleshy face, but he feigned cheeriness to cover his discomfiture.

"Not at all, not at all, doctor. Ah, you're too modest, you've kept me from seeing my friend's letter. The governor is one of my best friends."

"I was going to show it to you when I was ready to leave town, but since you just asked, here it is. Take a look," said Aslan, pulling a small letter out of his portfolio,

"Oh, thank you, thank you," exclaimed the pasha, taking the letter and reading it aloud:

Mr. Charles Rismane, the distinguished scientist and doctor who presents this letter to you, is about to visit Van in pursuit of his scholarly research and from there will be continuing on to India. I trust, gracious lord, that in carrying out my wishes you will be kind enough to make all the arrangements necessary to facilitate the fulfillment of his scientific purposes and ensure his comfort and safety in his travels, for which I will remain eternally grateful. . . . .

"This letter was written by my friend in his own hand," said the pasha after finishing it. "I'm fully prepared to facilitate your journey, doctor."

I sighed a sigh of relief, for I thought Aslan had extricated himself from his tight spot. Aslan then turned to Latif-Bek to satisfy his concerns as well:

"It's a good thing you reminded me to bring you the letter, sir. That will enable you to write a similar one for me. You might as well have it now, I'm so busy I may forget."

"Excellent," said Latif-Bek.

"Well, that's why I brought it. Here's my passport and the governor's letter. I trust these two items are all you need."

"They are," said the pasha. "This letter and ours will be ready for you just before noon tomorrow."

The Kurdish beg just sat where he was with a stony face. The prelate was left dumbfounded too. Even I wondered how Aslan had come by this letter. Aslan had described his itinerary quite honestly, and it was true that he was received with every necessary provision wherever he went and was seen off with a full escort. The only fact he withheld was that he had visited the monastery of the Holy Mother in the guise of an ascetic. Except for that, everything he had recounted was completely accurate.

Yes, he had acquitted himself quite well. But a cloud still hung over the Kurdish beg, and something had to be done to put him in a better light. He was the chief of the Jalali Kurds who had just committed the raids in question. Aslan knew it and said he would have to report it to the relevant officials. The matter could not simply be dropped.

This was the point at which Sharman-Bek, one of the Armenian notables, chimed in:

"You have to consider, doctor, that the latest raids by the Jalalis weren't against Turkish Armenians but against Persian Armenians."

"I know," Aslan responded curtly. "But an Armenian is an Armenian wherever he is, whether in Persia or Turkey. When he is robbed, the robber must be punished. It's not a question of nationality or jurisdiction, it's a question of criminality. If the victims had been Jews or Gypsies, I would protest even more."

Since Sharman-Bek's defense was found sorely lacking, the prelate weighed in:

"What you say is quite true, doctor, but you have to consider local practices and conditions. Such things happen all the time, marauding and stealing sheep and horses and so on. The only way you can get them back is by attacking Persian subjects."

"But how can peaceful Persian subjects be held responsible?" responded Aslan quite heatedly. "The marauders are always Kurds, whether they come from the Turkish or Persian side of the border. Let them take it out on each other if the local authorities can't control their bestial behavior. Why should innocent peasants be caught up in their clashes and trampled underfoot when all they have is a few animals to help them make a living?"

The Kurdish beg used his sleeve to wipe some beads of sweat from his brow, but it would be wrong to believe they arose from shame. On the contrary, he was consumed with his fury at a *gavour*[*] who had brazenly indicted him to his face when he couldn't pull out his sword and immediately dispatch him for his insolence. But he checked his rage and responded in measured tones:

"Doctor, I have the honor of being the leader of the Jalalis. Your low opinion of them is completely unjustified. If you knew half of what we've done for the Christians here you'd think differently."

"And I'd be only too happy to," responded Aslan with a courteous smile.

"I'd consider it unworthy to boast about myself," said the Bek, "But let the reverend caliph (the prelate) bear me out, he knows how much we've done."

The prelate then dutifully rendered a detailed account of all the contributions the Kurds had made to the country and particularly to the local Christians. Specifically in defense of the Jalalis, he cited the case a few weeks earlier in which the Bek himself had gone to the great festival of the Holy Mother of God to help keep order among the pilgrims. When the festival was over, it was the Bek's men who led the pilgrims safely back to their home districts and protected them from the dangers of the road.

---

[*]. A *gavour* is a non-believer, infidel, often used as a derogatory term against non-Muslims.

I was flabbergasted. It seemed that the hearts of all these men were bound together by some dark inner thread. They were masters of putting a good face on evil deeds.

If I and Aslan had not with our own eyes seen the Kurdish beg come to the festival to skim his portion of the pilgrims's donations to the monastery; if we didn't know the pilgrims had paid his men a great deal to protect them on their way home; if we didn't know that their fellow outlaws, with their knowledge, waited in hiding to ambush and rob the pilgrims on their way; if all of that hadn't been painfully clear to us, then without question we would have found the prelate's story entirely convincing. But, for obvious reasons, Aslan made no further response.

The interesting point in all of this was why the prelate had chosen to defend the Bek's barbarities. The prelate had close, friendly relations with almost all the Kurdish tribal chiefs and maintained them to augment his own power. The high level of power he had achieved was due to the influence he had over the country's worst outlaws. He therefore enjoyed the deference not only of the common folk but of the pasha himself. Yet couldn't such power have been put to better use? On one occasion, Aslan had said to me, "That man could be very helpful if he didn't use his position for evil purposes." There had been many cases in which one Kurdish leader or another had been thrown in prison or exiled for some crime. The prelate would provide large sums of money out of his own pocket to have them set free. Why? To turn them into his pliant tools.

The conversation touched once more on Aslan's departure the next day. The prelate took advantage of this opportunity to shift the focus of the conversation:

"Even though you'll have a letter from the pasha to ensure a smooth and safe journey, I'd advise you to travel in a caravan."

"That's just what I was planning to do. I heard a caravan will be setting out tomorrow evening," said Aslan.

"Whose caravan is it?" the prelate asked.

"I don't know," replied Aslan.

"It's Tokhmakh-Artin's caravan," volunteered the police chief.

"Ah yes, he's a hardy soul. His caravan will be the safest you'll find. But wouldn't you get bored on a caravan, doctor? Caravans move very slowly, you know," said the pasha.

"That's true," said Aslan. "But much as I'd like to hurry, I can only go so fast anyway because I have a big load to transport – my mobile pharmacy, my medical equipment, and all those antiquities I've collected. Besides that, I have to investigate several important historical sites, and the slow pace of the caravan will give me the chance to leave the main road and explore them at my leisure."

"Just make sure that when you do so you take plenty of men with you," advised the prelate.

"Of course, Reverend Father, I've had plenty of experience. Although this is my first time in your country, I've done a lot of traveling in central Asia."

Caravan

The countless fascinating stories that I had heard about caravans had always left me with the sense of something truly magical. You can therefore imagine how lucky I felt to join one for the very first time. Since traveling in the heat of day was out of the question, the caravan I was joining was due to leave town at sunset.

Varbed Panos and his entire family had come to see us off. Sadness could be read in all their faces, as if Aslan were one of their own family now setting off on a long journey that might never see his return. Aslan came down into the yard and shook hands all around and hugged the children. Our horses were waiting for us in the street, one a gift from the pasha to Aslan, and the other – a very fine steed – delivered from the caravan especially for me. Aslan embraced Varbed Panos one last time and I saw tears gleaming in the varbed's eyes as he watched us mount.

"Farewell friends," said Aslan.

"Happy traveling," responded the entire family.

With that we left this home full of gratitude, for it had offered us such hospitality, respect, and loving friendship.

Jahir Field in the vicinity of the town's parapets was the gathering place for all the travelers, and it was there we met khoja Toros for the last time. Certainly, reader, you won't have forgotten the identity of this Mosultsi tobacco merchant who dressed in Arab garb, this man with the keen and flashing eyes. . . We found him standing to one side talking with the leader of the caravan, and on seeing us he approached.

"Hello, doctor," he said, greeting Aslan and extending his hand. "I'm on my way, khoja Toros. What brings you here?"

"Well, what do merchants like me do? I have a load of cotton to ship to Bitlis and I brought it for the caravan to take. You're on your way to Bitlis, too, aren't you, doctor?"

"Yes, of course."

"And then on to Moush?"

"Definitely."

"Then, if you'd like, I can give you two letters of recommendation, one for Bitlis and one for Moush. I have good friends there, and they can give you a lot of help since you're interested in antiquities. That's right, isn't it, doctor?"

"Yes, thanks so much khoja Toros," said Aslan, taking the letters and shaking the Mosultsi's hand. With that we left to join the caravan.

Ah, caravans, the life of the East in motion! To see them is to see the East in its most vivacious and dynamic aspect . . .

Our caravan set out from *Jahir Field* at an hour when the crescent moons atop the minarets still caught the setting sun but before the mullah's call to evening prayers had been given. The caravan took up several leagues of the cramped, narrow road, the animals following behind each other in single file – a long living chain the end of which was out of view, advancing slowly, bending with the tight curves, twisting like a serpent, dropping down, then finding level ground again. . . .

All the animals in the caravan were mules. They followed along divided into teams of ten, each of a single color: white, black, dark brown, and so on. The white team was in the lead. Two servants accompanied each team to make sure the loads didn't tip or that in case one of the animals lost its footing and fell they could stand it up again. The mules were decked out from head to tail with the most colorful shells, beads, bouquets of flowers and small nut shaped bells. Every caravaneer took utmost pride in embellishing his animals, especially when setting forth from or drawing near a town. And these pampered animals were so accustomed to their adornments that they wouldn't take a step without them.

With the passing of hundreds of animals, the hills and mountains all around echoed with the tinkling of their bells, the sound taking on the rhythmic pattern of their tread and creating a totally magical effect, especially as they filed through desolate canyons in the middle of the night.

Out in front of the entire caravan was the *bishant*, the leader – a white, spirited mule with a broad chest and handsome head. Distinguished from all the others by his finer adornments, he is king of the mules and carries no load. He only leads.

Looking at that intelligent animal, I thought: How great would it be if those who were the leaders of this country and their lieutenants led with the same conscientiousness as this white mule?

The *bishant* is worthy of more description: Say it is winter, and all traces of road or path are covered in deep snow. The rough, uneven road is filled in, and a vast, level snowy expanse lies before you. A fragile horizon blends with an overcast sky. No matter which way you look, you see nothing, no sign of which way to go on the road. It's freezing cold, and the wind is driving the dense snow through the air. Terrified, you think the whole caravan is doomed, that it will vanish at any instant beneath a thick white blanket. And if you were passing through a desert, a windstorm would do the same work with sand as it does with snow in a blizzard. Every road would be buried in sand. No matter which way you looked, either to the sky above or the ground below, alas, a fine brown powder would have filled in everything. This is when the *bishant* saves you. As instinct incarnate, he finds the way no matter how buried it is. He will cut through snow with his mighty chest and lead the caravan forward. Even when everything is frozen and ice hangs from people's eyelashes, the *bishant*'s body is covered with a sweaty froth, and columns of hot air flow from his broad nostrils. And whenever he senses that he has found solid ground at last he stops, and the entire caravan comes to a halt behind him while he, with utmost concentration, turns his head this way and that. He cocks his ears and checks the direction of the wind. He looks up at the sky as if to determine the position of the stars. He puts his nose to the ground as if to catch the traces of some animal or other that has passed this way. And then, with a gentle whinny, he gives voice to his happiness and a wave of joy passes through the entire line of mules. They all whinny in chorus, for their leader has found the way; he has taken a new course and the whole caravan follows confidently behind. For the *bishant* there is no darkness in the night. His two eyes are lanterns leading him on. Whether in high mountains, through canyons, or along the edge of steep cliffs, with one wrong step he and the entire caravan may fall into a bottomless abyss. But he never takes a false step. It seems rather that his mighty hooves have eyes, and when from miles away he knows he is approaching an inn, again he whinnies joyfully and behind him all the other mules join in, whinnying and quickening their steps to arrive at last and take a rest.

The pack animals were in the lead, followed by the travelers who came along on horses or donkeys. The loads on these animals were even heavier. Two huge sacks containing provisions essential to traveling in Asia were slung over their backs: pots, pans, water, coffee making utensils, nargilehs with all their accessories, etc. Everyone had brought along his entire kitchen equipage with him and provided for himself. Without this precaution one ran the risk of starving on the trip, since in summer the caravan camped under open skies far from human settlements and in places where the animals could graze, since villagers would never permit them to graze in their vicinity. The traveler rides along comfortably seated on his bedding which is secured to the top of the carrying bags, the horse or mule barely visible beneath this enormous load.

Wealthier travelers ride on fully saddled and accoutred horses, with their servants and property, including tents, following behind on other horses. There were also women in the caravan, all wrapped in their shawls, their eyes and faces completely covered, riding on the horses like great balls of fabric. The wives of the rich rode in carriages pulled by pairs of mules.

The wealthy Muslim, even on long journeys, makes certain that he is lacking nothing. He is accustomed to smoking his nargileh whenever he wants or drinking coffee out of his thimble-sized cups, and for these indulgences a great deal is required: fire, water, and a variety of utensils, all in the care of his servants. On one side of his mule hangs an iron pot containing perpetually burning coals, like the fires of Ahura Mazda. On the other side is a leather water bag, for to a Muslim water is the most essential item, and he always carries his own. This is probably why these vessels have attained such a high level of workmanship in the East, and they keep the water cold and fresh even in the hottest conditions. This leather bag has all the advantages of a clay vase and allows ample contact between air and water. Also packed in the load are all the containers for keeping tobacco moist and the implements for making coffee. It's enough for the master merely to say the words "coffee" or "nargileh" for the servant immediately to make the coffee and prepare the nargileh for him. And you'd think the master were sitting in the middle of his home as he sits riding along with the end of the serpentine nargileh tube in his mouth, while the servant rides beside him holding the base.

There was also a group of Gypsies in the caravan, with their monkeys and dancing boys and girls. All of the boys and girls were well taken care of and rode on donkeys, while their masters went on foot. This gay ensemble of wanderers, with their constant laughter and endless antics, were the center of attention of the whole caravan.

There was also a group of Vanetsis in the caravan, laborers who having spent long years in foreign lands were now returning at last to their native villages. The time and distance that had separated them from home could be read in their sad faces, but the closer they drew the brighter their expressions. They trudged along with walking sticks in their hands and bedrolls on their backs, scorched and tanned by the sun. The Wandering Gypsy and The Wandering Armenian! Indeed, these two have much in common, the difference being that the former, as a citizen of the entire world, wanders the earth because he has no home, hearth, or fatherland to call his own, whereas the latter has all of those, yet is nevertheless forced to journey to distant lands to make a living. . .

The leader of the caravan was an Armenian, the well-known Tokhmakh-Artin from Erzeroum. Being an Erzeroumtsi, it was his habit at some point in any conversation to interject the statement, "Things have to get clouded before they get clear." It was for good reason that he had earned his name, Tokhmakh, for that is the name of the hammer a blacksmith uses to pound iron into shape. He was of medium stature and as solidly built as a tree trunk. Except for his nose and a small part of his forehead, his broad face was covered with hair, and even his ears were buried in thick, coarse hair. He used to say that his mother stole him out of a bear's lair. But as you talked to him the harshness in his face turned gradually softer, and his beauty showed through. Beneath his rough exterior lay a good and noble heart and the finest feelings. He rode a black horse, a rifle in his hand, his pistols tied to the saddle and a sword hanging from his belt. One moment he'd appear at the front of the caravan, then in a flash show up behind it. He was well acquainted with all the roads and passes and often rode off to the top of a hill to make sure there were no blockades or bandits ahead.

Tokhmakh-Artin was around fifty years old at this time but was still entirely youthful and vigorous. His more than twenty years of leading caravans had taken him from Asia Minor to Arabia, from Mesopotamia to Egypt, from the Caucasus to the Persian cities of Isfahan, Shiraz and Bandar-Busher. He was completely dependable, and merchants turned their gold shipments over to him without even bothering with any paperwork. When they got word that his caravan was due to arrive in their towns on such and such a date, they set everything else aside, no matter how important, and made sure to meet up with him in order to place their goods in his caravan. Artin was most renowned for one particular incident in which he was involved. This was when his caravan was attacked by hundreds of Bakhtiari bandits in the Lorris Desert. This occurred as his caravan was on its way toward the Persian Gulf. Artin was gravely wounded in the attack and lost several of his men in the ensuing battle. But merchants generally put up with incidents of this kind, knowing that either all their money had been unavoidably lost to the bandits, or in case any was left the caravaneer had every reason to keep it to himself.

In this incident, a Persian merchant from Hamadan had turned five thousand pieces of gold over to Artin to be transported to Baghdad. He was convinced that it had all been lost, but one year later Artin appeared at his door with the entire box of gold.

"What's that?" the merchant asked. "Your gold," answered Artin.

"You mean there's some left?" the merchant asked, not believing his own eyes.

At that Artin explained: During the attack on his caravan he had dropped the box of gold into a gully and covered it up with soil and rocks. When his wounds had healed and he was fully recovered several months later, he returned to the spot and retrieved it. If he was late in returning it to the merchant, this was solely due to the time it had taken him to recover from his wounds.

"Long life to you, Artin!" the merchant cried out and offered him part of the gold to keep for himself. Artin thanked him, but declined:

"Why give it to me? It was my job either to get it where you wanted or bring it back to you. If the bandits didn't get it all, that's your good luck."

Artin had maintained his magnanimity through a life filled with misfortune and poverty, but this latest incident had really put him to the test. He had lost most of his mules to a contagious disease and didn't have a *para* left. Everyone considered him bankrupt. But by some miracle, it seemed, he soon rebuilt his caravan and was once again plying the mountains of Erzeroum with over a hundred mules. Everyone who knew him was amazed and wondered where he had found enough money to do this, and people came up with all sorts of stories: Some said that he had found a large treasure; some said that his merchant friends had collected a large sum of money and given it to him to rebuild his caravan; others went further and hinted at some "hidden source" of wealth, etc. Which of these accounts was true is beside the point. Suffice it to say that at this point all his mules were of the finest, and he was reputed to be the foremost of the Erzeroumtsi caravaneers.

We reached Ardamed before night had completely descended over the countryside. A splendid city at one time, Ardamed was now only a splendid little village at two and a half hours distance from Van, situated on a broad, triangular highland which descends gradually to the shores of Lake Van.

Ardamed is very beautiful with its vast farms and breathtaking view of Lake Van. Eighteen centuries earlier, Ardashes the Second's home castle sat atop its heights, with mighty towers and parapets and the fragrant flower gardens in which his sweetheart, Lady Satenig, the lovely Alan maiden, took promenades with her maidservants. Eighteen centuries before that, the temple of the goddess Astghig stood at the crest of the hill, its pillared facade looking down on the broad blue sea, each day decked with fresh flowers from Armenian maidens who sought good fortune from her.

Aslan pointed out a spring beside the road which led to Vosdan, Paghesh,[*] Moush, etc. It was carved deep into a mass of rock to the height of a man and had ample space around it. Clear, cold water gushed from this rocky recess in volumes sufficient to power a watermill. It was here that Hagop Mdzpnah, St. Gregory the Illuminator's uncle, had come to quench his thirst sixteen centuries earlier on returning from his expedition to look for Noah's Ark on Mt. Ararat. Having been overcome by sleepiness half-way up the mountain, an angel took mercy on the old man and appeared before him. The angel told him that it would be impossible for him to reach the summit, but gave him a fragment of wood from the Ark. This satisfied the patriarch and he happily descended Ararat with the relic. On reaching Ardamed he stopped at this spring to drink. The mischievous maidens of Ardamed were at the spring drawing water when he arrived there. When they caught sight of this old man at the spring, they began to laugh at him. But the patriarch put a curse on the brazen girls, and all their black tresses turned white. From that day on, all the girls born in Ardamed had a patch of white hair on their heads as a sign of this event. . . .

When Aslan and I visited the spring, there were still Armenian girls drawing water there just as they used to do in ancient days. The caps on their heads were so densely sewn with coins that they resembled silver bowls. But it was getting quite dark by now, and I looked in vain to find any trace of white in the long braids that hung down their backs.

*. Paghesh or Bitlis.

Aslan pointed out Semiramis's famous river,[*] whose gigantic and mighty embankments had been described by Movses Khorenatsi. As for what its name had been in olden times, I don't know. Its water had burst forth from the lower slopes of Mt. Sar-Pulakh at the ten different spots where that most illustrious of queens had tapped the mountain core, and its water poured into the aqueduct that she had made and was carried more than fifteen miles into the countryside. The river flowed through Hayots Tsor all the way to Ardamed, at which point it forked out to irrigate far-flung farms and fields, then came back together with a mighty roar into well-built embankments and flowed to Van and its Aykesdan.

In the time of Ardashes the Second twelve centuries earlier, Ardamed had been the playground of Queen Semiramis. Following on a disastrous lover's quarrel with Ara this sybaritic queen sought in other young men the love he had denied her, and running after them throught the bowers and fragrant flower gardens of Ardamed bewitched them with the gleaming jewels of her necklace. A prominent elder of the time decided to put an end to the queen's magic and her brazen advances toward the young men who were the objects of her passion. One day Semiramis was bathing in her marble pool, her voluptuous body immersed in the crystal clear waters supplied by her high aqueduct, all her clothes and magical jewelry placed on the velvety grass in the shade of rose bushes at the side of the pool. Her hair was down and she was combing it, when like a thief in the night the old man approached and noticed her necklace lying on the ground.

Remembering its magical powers, he snatched it up and ran toward the Lake with it. The angry queen, her hair flying in the wind, ran after him, but, being unable to catch up with him in her ineffectual rage, she took a large rock, wrapped her hair around it and hurled it at the thief like a slingshot. The rock didn't hit him, but flew a great distance and finally landed in a canyon near Ardamed.

Meanwhile, the old man had reached the shore of Tadvan and dropped the magical necklace into its waters, and the land was finally liberated from the mischief of this licentious queen.

---

[*]. This was the famous aqueduct built during the reign of the famed Assyrian queen, Shamiram (Semiramis).

The bards of Ardamed composed songs on this subject, but all our frugal Khorenatsi tells us about it is just three words: "Semiramis's beads [into the] lake."

Aslan pointed out the rock that Semiramis had hurled at the old thief and said:

"Ask any Ardamedtsi, and he will tell you the whole tale. Delightful Ardamed has produced singers and poets like the wonderful Koghtnik, yet what has become of their works? This story has only survived in the oral tradition of the people, and they've kept it alive for over four thousand years. A people who keep their traditions alive like that will never die, traditions that have survived all the great blows of history. A people who doesn't forget its past will find a way of dealing with the present. Look around. Every stone, every ruin, every hill, every spring or brook tells you something about the past. That's where you'll find the greatness of the land and its people."

It would have been a sin to leave Ardamed without tasting its sweet and fragrant apples.

When we were setting off, I noticed a young girl sitting beside the road with a basket of apples in front of her. "Are those for sale?" I asked

She nodded her curly head of hair, stood up, and looked me straight in the eye.

"How much are they?" I asked.

"Five para " she answered. "Including the basket?"

"No, including me," the Ardamedouhi replied, displaying her wit.

Do you realize how much five paras are? Two kopeks. Two kopeks for a whole basketful of apples! I could barely tie up one quarter of them in my kerchief and left the rest.

"Give her a little more, this lovely little girl seems very poor," Aslan said to me.

On receiving a silver five ghouroush coin from me, she went up to Aslan and asked to kiss his hand.

"Where I'm from, men kiss the girl's hand," Aslan said and pressed her fingers to his lips.

The girl smiled, said thank you, and went off in her ragged clothes.

I noticed the sadness in Aslan's face, this being only the second time I had seen tears in his eyes. I was certain that he wouldn't kiss the hand of even the most beautiful princess, and yet that poor girl had touched his heart.

We mounted our horses and set forth on the road, carrying melancholy memories of Ardamed with us.

Ardamed is virtually the gateway to Hayots Tsor,[*] the land where Haik our forefather wrought his wondrous feats, and it is filled with Armenian churches, chapels, and many sacred spots. Rocks engraved with crosses still remained sadly strewn about.

As Aslan beheld all these historic sights and spoke of all the traditions attaching to them, he was carried away by rapture and had forgotten all about the caravan, which by now had continued its journey and left us a great distance behind. When I brought this to his attention, he replied:

"We'll leave now and catch up with the caravan, but you had to know all this."

Ardamed was full of Armenian churches, chapels, and sacred ruins. Rocks engraved with crosses had been removed from them by irreverent Muslims to build their houses, and now remained only as sad and heart-rending rubble. But I had seen many such ruins from the Christian era, and they didn't really interest me. What drew my attention were those chambers, those enormous caves carved into the rock. I found them inexplicable and mysterious. I was especially impressed by two great rocks with cuneiform letters engraved on their faces. How many centuries they had seen pass before them, and how many nations had come and gone, and yet they remained!

By now the caravan had left us far behind and gone a great distance in the cool of the night. And though our horses galloped at full speed the whole way, we barely caught up with it just after it had reached Ankgh River and was preparing to camp for the night. Servants were unloading the mules and stacking the bundles on each other to form walls. When everything was unloaded, they removed the saddles, curried, combed, and brushed the mules vigorously, wiped away their sweat, then, taking their rifles with them, led them away from the camp to an area where they could graze. The travelers gathered on the river bank with friends and arranged their belongings around them. They spread their quilts and rugs out on the tender grass and with great contentment sat down together. Some were doing their ablutions at the edge of the river in preparation for their prayers. Some, having already done their ablutions, were kneeling in prayer beneath the open sky, while others who had already finished this

---

*. Literally, "The Valley of Armenians."

rite were carefully fingering their prayer beads while waiting for their servants to prepare dinner. The Muslim fulfills his religious obligations with complete regularity even when traveling. Taking that into account, Artin the caravaneer, though a Christian, had arranged the itinerary of the caravan so that they could carry out their religious obligations at the proper times, a form of consideration very welcome to those who always constituted the majority of people in any caravan.

From every quarter one could hear prayer and religious song. I always found it a pleasure to hear Muslims reciting verses from the Koran. It always brought to mind the blazing deserts of Arabia from the midst of which the fiery Arabian prophet had emerged. What great power in a book! One book – a single well written book, with its lofty verse and wondrous language – had bound a large portion of the world to its religion. I looked with envy on those Muslims. There were some Armenians in the caravan, too, but they didn't immerse themselves in prayer. An Armenian only prays when led by a priest. Outside the walls of a church, he has no thought of God.

While dinner was being prepared, lamp light revealed happy faces which betrayed not even the slightest signs of fatigue. Many fires had already been lit, pots large and small were being brought to a boil. The smell of pilav, butter, and roasted meat filled the air to open one's appetite.

Some had already finished eating and were smoking their nargilehs, lying on their sides with their backs propped against pillows. Servants were preparing a stimulating coffee, and this is how it all seemed to me:

The entire caravan, a great gathering of pilgrims at a sacred site, all kindled with religious fervor, every heart purified, in everyone the spirit of all encompassing compassion awakened – the impulse to help others, to do good to one another; the wealthy inviting those less fortunate to share in their food, considering it unconscionable to enjoy their bounty alone while another less fortunate person looked on in need. The caravan had united them all, and out of many different elements one great family had taken form. There were singers, mullahs, dervishes, an ashough, and many gypsies in the caravan, all of them on their way to different places. Now they were all entertaining their respective audiences without the least expectation of material gain. All of them had found their own crowd. In one spot an effendi would be gravely listening to a mullah recounting the miraculous deeds of bygone caliphs. In another spot a dervish, the philosopher of the East, would be sitting on his ever present animal skin, putting a number of philosophical questions to his audience. In another place an animated ashough was launching into a long ballad which he would continue at every rest stop until it was completed. The youth of the caravan had gone off a good distance from the camp to listen to the gypsies playing and singing their songs. Still further off could be heard the tinkling bells of the animals as they grazed in the grass and the singing of those who were watching over them. And from nearby – very near – the river was singing with its soft, sweet gurgling. All of these elements joined together in the stillness of the night to produce the most delightful and soul-stirring harmony.

As for Artin, he was still on his feet, constantly going from one group to another, asking how they were, making sure everyone's needs were being met, then leaving them with words of cheer. He received warm invitations from all around, but graciously declined, saying that he still had a great deal to do.

I and Aslan were observing this entire scene from where we sat at the river's edge when suddenly Artin appeared and greeted us with his usual cordiality:

"Hello, doctor. Unless you want to go completely hungry, please do me the honor of joining me for supper. I don't believe you brought any food along."

And, to be sure, it was a fact that we hadn't given a thought to bringing any food along, reasoning that the caravan would be stopping near human settlements, and that we could therefore find whatever we needed there. But in actuality, all one could expect to find in any village would be barley flour bread and eggs. Aslan seemed to be waiting for Artin's invitation. He thanked him and followed as Artin led the way to his tent.

Artin's white tent was so large it could accommodate a number of families. And it wasn't lacking in a certain grace. It would seem that this "man of the wild," as he liked to call himself, had his own unique taste in finer things. When I kidded him about this, he replied:

"Good Lord, I've been living without a roof over my head for thirty years. I've spent my whole life in canyons and mountains and deserts. This tent has been my only consolation. You should realize that it isn't so much for me as for my travelers. They find shelter here when it's extremely hot or when it rains."

"Just like us," I added. "But do you also feed them all?"

"If they're poor and have nothing to eat, I do. Sometimes I take in sick people who need rest and care. They're always welcome into my tent until they've reached their destination."

After we had eaten, Aslan asked Artin:

"How are the roads here?"

"Always bad," said Artin. "Was there ever a time when they weren't? Take this spot, for example. We're not very far from towns here. The village of Antgh is just half an hour away, but this is one of the most dangerous spots we're sitting in now. If you go out and take a good look around you'll find a bandit behind every rock, in every gully, under every bush. We caught one of them just a short time ago. And guess what, it was a woman!"

"Very interesting," said Aslan.

"Yes, the little devils are more dangerous than their husbands. They slip across the river in the dark and sneak up on a caravan like a fox to a chicken house. Then they run up to a trunk of goods, quickly cut it open with their sharp knives, and off they go with its contents. They're totally invisible."

"So what did you do with the woman you caught?" I asked

"What could I do? I pulled her hair a couple of times and turned her loose."

"And what would you have done if it had been a man?"

"That would've been different."

"Aren't you afraid?"

"What's there to be afraid of? They're flesh and blood like me, not iron."

"But they're wild."

"Cowardly beasts, believe me, very cowardly. That's the way all wild people are. I've seen plenty of them, and I've had plenty of dealings with them. How can a barbarian have courage, someone whose only ideal is to plunder as much as he can?"

"That's really true," Aslan observed after listening carefully to everything Artin had said. "True courage involves a sense of self-sacrifice, but that feeling doesn't exist without the highest ideals."

Having made these comments, Aslan fell silent again. This was his first chance to get a real rest after all his hard work in Van, and he retired unusually early. Good Lord, he was in such an overwrought state he could barely relax!

I lay on my bed unable to fall asleep. The image of Tolakh-Artin hovered before my mind's eye – that dusky, hirsute image, those black and fiery eyes. Artin was clearly not a man given to empty boasting. Everything he recounted, every episode was all too real. He was, in fact, a man who knew no fear. From the many stories I had heard about him, what truly stood out in all of them was his bravery. A caravaneer can't afford to be a fearful man, for he is constantly confronted with any number of dangers. But there was more to Artin than bravery alone. He could have commanded an entire regiment, yet he was humane. In all his actions what shone through was a powerful inclination toward goodness and kindness. I was incredibly impressed by the level of moral purity he had retained, for caravaneers are ordinarily so calloused from their routine dealings with animals that, on the moral plane, they're barely a cut above them. But with Artin, caravaning had become almost an art, and I was deeply impressed by the order and harmony that prevailed in his caravans.

The lamps were being extinguished one by one as all activity came to a halt. A profound silence reigned in the caravan. There was only the melancholy sound of the river to be heard, and in it I thought I could hear the story of what had transpired here four and a half millenia before. . .

The Seer

When we at last descended from Haik's Fortress Aslan mounted without a word and set out toward the southern side of Hayots Tsor and the Rshdunik mountains. His two companions already knew where he was headed and turned their horses to follow him. I fell in behind.

All of us were still under the powerful sway of the impressions left on us by our visit to the ancient fortress and we went a long way without speaking. It was early afternoon and the sun was beating down, heating up hill and plain. It felt like being baked in an oven. In that kind of extreme heat your sweat pours out and coats your face with a thick layer of salt; your lips crack and your eyes burn.

Millions of nearly invisible insects swarm around your head, ready to fill your mouth and nose when you breathe in. They fill your eyes and buzz in your ears and there's no escape.

Such extreme heat inflames the imagination, as well. I looked up at the sky and, good Lord, what fantastic visions I saw: a whole monastery suspended in the sky, with its domes and belfries and trees all around. Looking off into the distance toward Lake Van, I thought I saw a band of armed and mounted angels making their rounds in the heavens and a vast flock of sheep grazing there in mountain pastures. What in the world was happening? I thought for a moment of asking our guides about it, since they were familiar with the land and might be able to explain my strange experiences, but they'd only have laughed and taken me for a lunatic. When I reported my visions to Aslan some time later, he gave me a complete explanation of the natural phenomena that had produced them, and I was amazed at what a remarkable thing true science is and what an array of superstitions it can dispel.

Off in the distance a number of black dots could be seen at the foot of the Ardos mountains, some Kurdish tents. The twilight bathed them in a reddish purple light so that they almost seemed to be flaming. The sun was setting and the darkness crept in until the marvelous sight vanished in endless night and all that could be seen was the glimmer of fires beckoning to us.

Aslan told me that this camp belonged to a very important Kurdish sheikh, a man who wielded tremendous influence over all the Kurdish tribes and was nearly regarded as a prophet. All the Kurds swore by his name. When he was finished with his bath, his followers would take his bath water and rub it into their beards like holy water.

"But he's an extreme fanatic and a terrible enemy of all Christians," Aslan continued. "He's so hostile to Christians that he covers his face when he travels from one place to another so that none of them get a glimpse of his sacrosanct countenance. He's been responsible for destroying countless monasteries and burning scores of Armenian villages to the ground. He enjoys nothing more than annihilating Christians."

"What's he doing here?" I asked

"He ran into trouble in Persia a few months ago and came here to hide out for awhile."

"What kind of trouble?"

"He led his army on raids through several districts along the southeastern shores of Lake Urmia."

"Is he that powerful?"

"Of course. He can pull together an army of ten or twenty thousand in a single day if he wants to."

"Where is he from?"

"From the Zab River Valley, not far from Albak and Jolamerik. He's very rich and owns vast estates and villages there."

"And all that wealth comes from plunder?"

"Completely."

"But why are you going to visit such a notorious criminal?"

"I'm not. I want to see someone else."

"But do you and the Sheikh know each other?"

"Yes, but he wouldn't recognize me in my European clothing."

It was quite late at night when we reached the camp. The campfires had died down and it was completely dark. There were large numbers of horses, sheep, cows and oxen all around, giving the appearance of a temporary pastoral camp, but this was a camp that in the twinkling of an eye could spring into action as a full-fledged army. Night watchmen were posted all around the periphery and there was no way to get by them unnoticed. Watchdogs sprang out of the darkness and lunged ferociously at our horses as we approached. This caught the attention of the night watchmen and they asked us what our business was.

"We've come to see The Seer," Aslan answered.

"He's over there," one of them said, pointing to a solitary tent at the far edge of the camp.

"The Seer," as he was known, was in such demand among the Kurdish populace that he might receive visits from them morning, noon, or night and therefore our appearance at that untimely hour came as no surprise to the watchmen.

When we arrived at his tent we found him alone, sitting inside reading a book in the lamplight. He put down his book at our approach and came out to greet us.

"How goes it?" he asked.

"Quite well, thank heaven," said Aslan. "We've come for you to tell our fortune."

The Seer stood at the entrance to his tent like a white statue, his long white hair flowing down and blending with his beard. He was clothed in a white tunic that descended to his bare feet and resembled the liturgical garments used in the Armenian church. He really couldn't see how we were dressed or what ethnic group we belonged to, but that was unnecessary to him, for he welcomed everyone equally.

"Please dismount and come inside," he invited us. "But you'll have to take care of your horses yourselves, because I'm alone and don't have anyone to help."

Our guides were fully prepared to take care of the horses on their own. They took the fetters out of their saddlebags and secured the horses with them so they wouldn't wander off.

The Seer sat back down in the corner of the tent near his books, and Aslan and I sat down on either side of him. "It seems we interrupted your studies," said Aslan apologetically.

"Oh, I've got plenty of time to read," said The Seer. "The most important thing now is to entertain the guests that God has sent my way."

The Seer was very famous. People came bearing gifts from far and wide to see him about their personal problems. He gave away the gifts he received to the poor and went on living in complete poverty. The Sheikh himself had great respect for him and sought his counsel in almost all his most important decisions. It was said of The Seer that once a year he disappeared into a cave for forty days at a time, going without food or drink for the entire period and while there communing with spirits and having heavenly visions.

In the lamplight I could see the vestiges of a once proud face, but age and self-mortification had lent his expression a kind and righteous look. Nevertheless, at one point when he swept the hair back from his brow I was shocked to see a terrible, reddish scar on his forehead, the kind that death row prisoners are branded with, and suddenly his face took on a fearsome look. Some explained the scar by saying that he had at one time ended up in the clutches of infidels who had branded him this way.

Aslan inquired about the book The Seer was reading when we arrived.

"It's a theological book in Arabic," he answered. "Very few Kurds, even the spiritual leaders, know how to read Arabic. But I've mastered the language and have read many books in it. I started learning it when I was already an old man, even though it would take a whole lifetime to learn it well. The Sheikh respects me deeply for my ability to read Arabic and often asks me to deliver sermons for him."

"So then, I take it you're one of his closest advisors," said Aslan.

"You could say so. The people regard me as his right hand man, but I'm obliged to be modest about that. Honor and status are nothing to me. This humble tent is all the reward I need."

Just at that point in the conversation one of our guides came in to ask Aslan if he was ready to have a meal, but when his and The Seer's eyes suddenly met an extraordinary thing happened. The two men were totally stupefied on getting a good look at each other, then like a father and son who had long been separated they sprang toward each other and embraced, sighing and muttering with incredible emotion.

"Kavor Bedros!" the young man cried out, standing back and looking at The Seer. "Oh Mourad! Dear Mourad!' the old man said in a trembling voice.

I was totally taken aback, and what further amazed me was that the two of them were speaking to each other in Armenian, because up to that point all the conversation between Aslan and The Seer had been in Kurdish. But Aslan remained cool and collected and, like the responsible physician he was, helped the old man sit back down in his place to prevent his having some kind of seizure.

"Dear God!! Who could have predicted this!" the young man said.

"Ah, Mourad, my dear child. You've found me once more in highly suspicious circumstances, and who could blame you for believing that I'm just the same as I always was, a criminal and cross-thief and still up to my old ways? Ah, if you only knew what forced me to continue in this shameful ruse, you'd forgive me, good lad that you are, and you'd understand."

"And he'd still love you," said Aslan.

"Yes, I'd still love you, and I do love you," the young man said, taking The Seer's hand in his. "I understand you. I know that no matter how many good deeds you do, you still feel you'll never make up for all your crimes. But that's all in the past now. Your present self-sacrifice will wipe the slate clean, because you're serving a higher purpose."

"My old crimes, indeed!" the old man exclaimed, wiping away some tears. "Is there enough mercy in heaven to forgive me for them? Even though I repented long ago, I've given up any Christian hope of salvation in the next life. Let me go to hell. Let everlasting torture be my lot. Even if new crimes are added to my old ones, I'll see my task through, no matter what."

"We used all of our talents and abilities to pursue nothing but our own selfish, evil interests," the young guide said. "But just who were 'we'? We were the face of an entire people mired in degeneracy. We were blind to the higher and inviolable needs of society as a whole. We turned our backs on our obligations to our nation, to our homeland, and to humanity itself. Instead, we became parasites and were branded 'cross-thieves'; not just ordinary thieves, but men who stole what was most precious and sacred to people. We stole their lives, their property, their honor without conscience but still never got enough. All our crimes were successful and only inspired us to commit more. But the time has come for us to come clean, to put away the old man and as new men to work for the good of all."

The Seer was deeply moved and planted a kiss on his forehead on hearing these words, words that issued from the lips of a man I had taken to be merely a rough and simple muleteer. When he rose to his feet Aslan gave me a sign that it was time for me to leave the tent. Mourad and I went out and settled down near the horses a good distance from the tent, leaving Aslan and The Seer alone. I had no idea what they would be talking about and couldn't hear a word, but their conversation continued well into the night and the lamps inside the tent continued burning until the dawn.

The cool night air was very soothing after a whole day spent under the punishing sun. A refreshing breeze blew from the direction of Lake Van, bearing along the incredibly sweet scents of the Ardos mountains. But the sky was clouded over, without the trace of a star. Large raindrops came down from time to time and lightning flashed in the distance from the direction of Haik's Fortress, as if the Armenian and Babylonian giants of old were still battling it out, flailing the mountainsides with their mighty clubs.

Mourad and Jallad were busy with the horses, covering them with blankets to protect them from the impending rain. I lay in the grass staring up at the impenetrable gloom. It was dark, so dark, everything lost in darkness like the dismal future of the country. . .

All I could see before my mind's eye was The Seer, and his enigmatic words kept echoing in my brain. There must have been some explanation for them, but none came to me. I had just the two names, Mourad and Kavor Bedros, to go by, but that offered a beginning. Those two were infamous cross-thieves from Salmast and notorious there as masters of that illicit profession. I had heard countless amazing tales about them from my childhood. . .

All during our journey I had been troubled by the feeling that I had seen Mourad somewhere before, and I wasn't wrong. Little by little the mystery started clearing up for me.

Do you remember, dear reader, that sad and stormy night when I escaped from Der-Todik's school? Do you remember how I wandered through the old town in despair, not knowing where to go; how Garo suddenly appeared out of nowhere and led me to the ruins of the old minaret where I met his other comrades, Aslan and Sako? Mourad and Jallad were also there for a short time, but when morning came they were gone. But now, many months later and under very different circumstances, our paths had crossed again. I was extremely surprised to discover that the two of them had taken jobs as muleteers in Erzeroumtsi Artin's caravan. Why had they done so, and what common bond brought them and Aslan in league with Artin? Who really owned the mules? These questions swept me into a jumble of confusion and all kinds of fantastic conjectures vied with each other in my mind. . .

Mourad and Kavor Bedros, names that had filled me with trepidation! And I was shocked that Aslan would have anything to do with such notorious cross-thieves. But when I reflected on the moving scene that had just transpired between them only a few minutes earlier; when I remembered the deeply emotional words that Mourad had uttered, the darkness began to dissolve and a bright new horizon opened up before me as I glimpsed the possibility that even the vilest of criminals could repent and dedicate himself to the service of the greater good. It occurred to me, also, that it wasn't just a Salmastsi or a Savratsi who can be a cross-thief, but even a priest, a merchant, a teacher, a vartabed or a lofty official, as well; and further, even an entire nation can be a cross-thief if it has reached the depths of immorality and places all its abilities and capacities at the service of evil.

By the time Mourad finished his tasks and came back and sat down beside me I finally remembered seeing him at the Arabian minaret. I was sure he remembered me, too, but he didn't let on because he had confidence in his disguise as a Laz tribesman and because the last time we had met he was dressed as a Zeitountsi and spoke in the Zeitountsi dialect.

In any case, I thought it best not to breach the matter. Nevertheless, I thought I could get him to talk about his relationship with Kavor Bedros, since I had witnessed the entire emotional scene between them.

"You must have known Kavor Bedros for quite awhile," I ventured. "I didn't just know him, he was my teacher."

"That old cross-thief?"

"Yes."

"How did you end up with him?"

"That's a long, long story; it would take all night to tell."

"But please tell me. I've heard so much about him."

"Well, then, you must have heard my name, too."

"Yes, because your name was always mentioned together with his."

"Of course. Our names were completely inseparable from each other."

Mourad then recounted how he had been apprenticed as a young boy to Kavor Bedros to learn the blacksmith's trade. Very soon after he had begun his apprenticeship, Kavor Bedros suddenly came under the suspicion of the authorities in Persia for committing a major crime, and

Mourad being his pupil fell under suspicion, as well, and was forced to flee his home and the clutches of the law to save his life. He then encountered a band of young men who had taken refuge in a forest near Savra and, like him, were escapees from Der-Todik's school. Among them were Garo, Aslan, and Sako, and he had remained in the forest with them for many weeks. From time to time they received visits from an old hunter whose name was Avo, and he gave them wise counsel and guidance on what they should do with their lives. But Mourad wasn't able to linger for long with this group due to a certain development and ended up in Kavor Bedros's hands. Kavor Bedros took him into foreign lands and carefully trained him in all the skills of a cross-thief, while in the case of Garo, Aslan, and Sako, they also ended up in foreign lands but received advanced educations and became respectable men. What a remarkable story! The story of a wandering people subjected to all the trials of a merciless fate, a people in whose history each individual could see his own clear reflection. . .

"Then you've known Aslan and his friends since childhood," I observed when he had brought his account to an end.

"Yes, from an early age," Mourad answered. "But our ways parted and we went in opposite directions. While Hunter Avo led the others toward the good, Kavor Bedros ushered me into a life of crime. Nevertheless, after all that time our paths have come full circle and we've been able to reach out to each other again."

"But how did you change and turn from your life of crime?"

"I got caught in my crimes one day and was sent to Siberia. While I was a prisoner there I became acquainted with a very fine man, a fellow prisoner.

He deeply influenced me and set me on the right path."

"Who was he?"

"They called him 'The Mute,' because he hardly ever said a word. To this day I don't know his real name. He was a very mysterious person."

"What became of him?"

"I never found out."

At that moment Mourad's companion reappeared after a long trek in search of grass to feed the horses, and I asked Mourad to introduce us.

"I believe you're already acquainted with him. You saw him with me at the Arabian minaret back then. Don't you remember?"

"Yes I do. I remember both of you," I admitted at last. "His name is Jallad, isn't it?"

"Yes, Jallad."

So now there were no longer any secrets between us; we were old comrades.

Aslan called out from the tent that the horses should be prepared for departure. When they were ready, the old Seer came out to see us off and give us his benediction, saying, '*Hachoghoutyoun!*[*] as we rode off at first light. This was the send-off we always received from our comrades when we parted. The sheikh's camp still lay in deep slumber, while the night guards around the periphery continued exchanging their signals with each other as we left.

When we had reached the main road, Mourad warned us, "From this point on we'll be passing through some very dangerous country, so have your weapons at the ready."

Mourad took the lead and Jallad brought up the rear, with me and Aslan safely between them. The trail was extremely challenging and dropped steeply into the intersecting crevices and canyons of the Ardos, a yawning trap into which a man could in the twinkling of an eye fall and disappear forever. The interlacing of the Ardos and Gaboudgogh ranges formed the backbone of Rshdounik. We rode through forest after forest and frequently crossed paths with nomads driving their herds to pasture. We were totally hemmed in by the mountains and that made me very uneasy. I couldn't wait to get out of there and see the light of day again. I could only guess that the sun had risen by now, judging by the golden glow on one side of the snow-white clouds that drifted overhead. But it was still dark all around us. The sun didn't penetrate these canyons even on the brightest of days, and everything was still shrouded in the morning mist. We were exhausted at this point but had gone through the most dangerous part of our trek. When we at last reached the top of a mountain it was with a great deal of relief that I looked off in the distance and glimpsed the azure expanse of Lake Van.

"Look, there's Vosdan!" exclaimed Aslan, pointing out some ancient ruins in the distance.

Vosdan! A name familiar to me from childhood! Not a name I had read about in books but one I used to hear in the lullaby mothers sang to

---

[*]. "*Hachoghoutyoun*" = "Success [to you]" in Armenian.

their babies as they rocked them back and forth to put them to sleep, a song that promised them all kinds of gifts when they grew up: gleaming weapons made of silver, clothes of gold filigree, spirited horses, and so on. Each line of the lullaby ended with the refrain, "And where, oh where, will I find them for you? In Van and in Vosdan!"

That song was part and parcel of Vosdan's glorious past, and whenever I heard it I pictured a vast, thriving city, full of all the world's riches. But what a disillusionment it was to see these ruins! Nothing was left of Vosdan but a handful of miserable cottages occupied by a few pathetic Kurds.

So I wondered why Aslan had brought us here; why he always led us from one depressing set of ruins to another. Was there nothing else to see in this land, anything that one could take pleasure in?

Smoke was rising up from the roofs of the subterranean Kurdish cottages. Some dogs started barking at us and a number of children, women, and girls slipped out of narrow openings onto their roofs to look at us. We then saw an old man hobbling toward us on a pair of crutches. Though Kurds are generally very civil, he offered no greeting but instead cast a suspicious look at us. This may have been because Muslims have a whole range of greetings they use with strangers, depending on their perceived rank, ethnic origin, or religious persuasion, and that he was uncertain which greeting to use. We at first took him for a mere beggar but, his tattered clothing notwithstanding, one soon noticed signs of exceptional dignity in him. Stuck in his sash was a small pistol with an ebony handle elegantly inlaid with silver and multicolored, precious gems, sufficient proof of his aristocratic status.

"Do you have any tobacco," he asked, finally breaking his silence.

"Yes, we do," said Mourad in perfect Kurdish, handing him a generous amount. The old Kurd immediately set to smoking as if it had been ages since he had enjoyed tobacco.

He then turned around and hobbled back to his cottage. In about fifteen minutes he re-emerged accompanied by a man carrying a large basket piled high with freshly baked bread and broad slabs of herb cheese for us. He set it before us and we began to eat.

"Which tribe are you from?" Mourad asked the old aristocrat. "The Vroushiks," he answered proudly.

"Oh, the Vroushiks!" said Mourad, quite impressed. "Did you know that your ancestors were Armenian?"

"I don't know any such thing," the old man replied somewhat crossly. "All I know is that my ancestors built that fortress over there."

"Exactly, and they were Armenians. They called themselves 'Rshdounik' and their land was known by the same name. Your tribe grew out of those people, just as the Kurdish tribe of Mamgani grew out of the Mamigonian dynasty. And there are many other Kurdish tribes of Armenian origin."

"Perhaps so," the old man responded skeptically. "All of us were brothers at one time, but then the devil came and sowed discord among us and forced us to speak different languages so that we couldn't understand each other."

"You mean in the times of Adam and Noah."

"No, I mean during my own lifetime. I'm talking about what I know and saw myself. It's true, as you say; that fortress once belonged to the Ghara-Melik Armenian princes, and we were good friends with them in those days. We used to go into battle side by side against our enemies and when it was over we divided the spoils equally with each other. But then Satan came and led my father's brother astray. He invited the Melik and his men to dinner one day and had them all killed as they were eating."

"And so – don't you see what came out of that?" said Aslan, intervening in the conversation. "By killing your former friends you were left weak and alone. Then you too were destroyed soon after. You dishonorably took over the fortress that had belonged to your friends, but you weren't able to keep it. The Ottomans came and took it away from you. If you had remained loyal to your friends none of that would have happened."

"That's true, so true," the old Kurd answered with a sadness he couldn't hide. "But who set us against each other and made us betray each other? It was the Ottomans. They came and sowed the seeds of suspicion among us and forced us to betray each other. I haven't told you the half of it, all the secretive ways the Ottoman agents incited us against the Armenians. But we were too stupid to see through it and understand they were preparing to destroy us, too, the first chance they got."

"And they're still doing it, isn't that so?"

"Yes, and in even more terrible ways. But our aristocrats still don't understand; neither do our spiritual leaders. Right now, not far from here, a famous sheikh is camping at the foot of the Ardos. You've probably heard something about him. He is a man of God and it would be a great shame for me to question it, but he is very impetuous. The Ottomans have incited him against the Armenians time and time again and he's laid waste to many of their districts. Yet all the Kurds heed him and obey. All he has to do is wake up one morning and say the Prophet appeared to him in a dream and ordered him to go forth and slaughter all the gavours. The Kurds will immediately grab their weapons and follow him wherever he leads. If it weren't for The Seer, he would do worse things still."

"Who is this 'Seer' you're talking about?" asked Aslan, with feigned ignorance.

"They say he came from Arabia, the Prophet's native land. He's very holy and knows everything there is to know. He can answer any question you ask. Even the Sheikh goes to him with many questions."

RAFFI

ARMENIA'S FOREMOST NOVELIST

Authentic, first rate translations into English

www.gomidas.org * *info@gomidas.org*

Gomdas Institute
42 Blythe Rd.
London W14 0HA

www.ingramcontent.com/pod-product-compliance
Lightning Source LLC
Chambersburg PA
CBHW051144020726
47501CB00005B/1674